THE EDWARD DOUGLASS WHITE
LECTURES ON CITIZENSHIP

MORALITY
and
ADMINISTRATION
in
Democratic Government

By

PAUL H. APPLEBY

GREENWOOD PRESS, PUBLISHERS
NEW YORK

To

MARGARET, MARY ELLEN, L. TOM,

THEIR CHILDREN, AND THEIR WORLD.

PREFACE

FOR THE THIRD time an agreement at the meeting of a professional society to give a series of lectures has involved me in the somewhat dubious business of producing a book written around lectures. This particular occasion, the Edward Douglass White Lectures at Louisiana State University, saw the duty fully compensated in a spring visit to that beautiful campus, the pleasure of association with its faculty, and the evidence of excellent work being done there.

A personal desire to give special attention to ethical considerations in public administration, and the interest of many colleagues in political science, led to the choice of topic. "Morality" was selected for use in the title in preference to "ethics" to avoid the suggestion that either a treatment in the systematic terms of general philosophy or a "code of administrative ethics" was to be attempted. These considerations point to the basic difficulty of the task, which involves the relating of all manner of specific governmental actions in highly varied work situations to abstract, philosophical thought.

The difficulty is compounded by consideration of probable audiences for the oral and written versions, representing mixtures of undergraduate and graduate students, mature scholars in several fields, and administrative practitioners. To present in brief compass a discussion bearing on wideranging action related to some of the profoundest problems of social concern is to attempt a feat so difficult as to be presumptuous. Justification is found simply in the present rarity of efforts to deal with this relationship and in the need further to emphasize the value content of public administration.

Ethical problems of the public administrator range from the very small, particular, and personal to those bearing in important and highly complicated ways upon the nature of an unfolding democracy. The simpler problems I have considered here somewhat incidentally in order to focus attention chiefly on the more fundamental value-concerns. There are many assumptions and many affirmations which may be for others hypotheses requiring extended examination. Here, as in other writings, my intention is to insist upon what practitioners feel is the reality, in the hope that other critical discussions may be more often related to improvement of the reality and less often merely negative, fearful, vague, unrealistic, remote. The great need is to stimulate the interest of competent scholars in bringing theory up to date, clearly and adequately bearing on the actual business of carrying on government with popular character and popular understanding in a volatile world speeding into ever vaster complexity. Administration is an important area to be comprehended in any adequate modern theory.

With these considerations in mind, I have made no attempt to meet the expectations of readers to whom the title of this book will suggest a direct and specific discussion of such indefensible wrongdoing and improprieties as were much publicized in 1951. The worst of these disclosures focused on metropolitan government, which presents problems of such variety and special character as to require separate and different treatment from that attempted here. In this book I deal with the generality of government as distinguished from private activities, and particularly with the national government. Here, therefore, will be found nothing bearing pointedly on the Kefauver Committee investigations.

Similarly, no specific reference is made to disclosures during the same year of serious lapses on the part of national officials. These revelations do indicate a disturbing impairment of strict standards earlier more uniformly obtaining. They indicate also the corrective processes and sanctions which the more sophisticated or more experienced personnel anticipated and guarded against, and it may be believed that the result of them will be highly educational, preventive of further laxity, and actually uplifting of practice throughout the government. In less dramatic ways, a similar process of correction goes on less spasmodically in the course of normal administration.

Even in 1951, the general affirmations of comparative virtue found in the pages of this book deserved credence, although many readers will not believe them and others will misunderstand their terms. The very outrage of the public over relatively few cases of really established corruption of administrative decisions, and over some relatively mild if wholly inexcusable indiscretions, points to the peculiar elevation of public expectations with respect to the national government. Such expectations can not be wholly apart from the practice to which the public is habituated. The whole affair really testified to the relative elevation of normal practice at the national governmental level. This is true even though other similar revelations might be expected from other areas of the governmental scene. The more likely places would be in the corporations and other atypical governmental structures. With the full story told, however, cases even suggestive of impropriety would have involved a microscopic fraction of the national government's personnel.

The points of responsibility for the derelictions that were

brought to light were in the offices of amateurs in governmental responsibility. The most serious locus was in the
Bureau of Internal Revenue, and there, in the persons of
political appointees. The point should not be confined to
association of this fact with patronage, although putting the
collectors under civil service will be importantly corrective. Many good "political" appointments are made, more
could be made, and political appointments at and around
heads of agencies are essential to the reality and effectiveness of democratic government. One of the sources of trouble has been in keeping open to patronage the wrong kind
of jobs; not many have remained thus open, and the posts
of collectors have provided one of the most serious examples. A more basic source of trouble has been in the lack
of suitable criteria for selection outside of civil service, a
lack of citizens with understanding of the peculiar responsibilities of public service, and the resulting tendency of
many appointees to take into government mores of the
private economy.

Practices wholly inappropriate in government have never
been similarly scrutinized and publicized, and are not on
the whole so thoroughly out of place, in private life. In
business, it is a universal practice to try to develop friendly
relationships as at least marginally determining the channel-
ing of purchases. In many ways, impersonal and objective
business competition is watered down by personal and institutional interaction. Receipt of gifts usually goes unre-
marked. I recall the case of a citizen who, while he served
as president of a certain corporation, received annually at
Christmas from business "friends" gifts which literally filled
his large house. He was shocked by the practice only when,
after his retirement, the gifts ceased to come. The appointment of such a person to a public position would have been

widely applauded, yet he could hardly have failed to make himself vulnerable in a public post.

Another source of governmental trouble is the sudden elevation to a highly influential place of some loyally congenial but unqualified intimate of a high official, or the similar elevation of a civil servant or expert into a highly charged political exposure and function. With neither political nor administrative competence appropriate to the new post such men can unwittingly act so as to encourage laxity in ways that would be scorned by a hard-boiled and broadly experienced politician. The rather accidental presence of a few such, and the not unrelated presence of some business-type patronage appointees—amateurs all in public responsibility—was the occasion for an unknowing opening of the door to conditions which became rather suddenly revealed in 1951.

Nevertheless, with respect to this kind of moral lapse, standards of the national government remained in 1951 higher than standards outside it, generally characterized by diverse and complicated preventive practices and by high devotion to public values. Blots on that particular record revealed in one spasm of correction should not direct attention away from matters more profound and difficult.

These other matters weigh heavily on the most intelligent, competent, and devoted of public officials, and require appreciation and understanding of citizens. For introductory illustration, two rather typical problems facing the Forest Service may be cited. That organization, having responsibility for "sustained yield-use" of perhaps two billions of dollars worth of our natural resources, grants to private persons permits for grazing and lumbering operations and enforces conservation. Over a period of time some cattlemen develop large enterprises based in crucial part on grazing permits. A truly competitive situation rarely exists, and tends to be eliminated almost altogether. Sudden and drastic reduction of the grazing permitted to single large operators would have devastating effects on them, but failure to open the resources to new applicants of small size would be inequitable. What is sound and fair public policy in each of many thousands of such situations is a question of heavy moral content and great practical difficulty.

Similarly, the Forest Service must weigh the practical program needs of the user cattlemen altogether, and the user lumber suppliers, altogether, as against the public need for conservation of the ranges and forests. The public is for the most part far away, while the users are near, insistent, and influential.

There are important conflicts of values in these administrative problems, and the conflicts relate to the whole structure and process of public administration, as well as to the more general structures and processes of politics and society. Such matters are peculiarly public-organizational problems, having to do with complicated organizational conduct under public responsibility. I would direct attention to such things.

Attempting so to do, in these pages I show a personal preference for the word "organization" as contrasting with the sociological "association" or "institution," feeling that it is the stronger word and more suggestive of administration.

Also, there has been some yielding to a sense of need to repeat, as relevant and essential to the present discussion, certain things I have said elsewhere descriptive of organizational performance.

Indebtedness is gratefully acknowledged to a good many persons. Some of these have read and commented upon the entire manuscript, some have reviewed particular chapters, and others have helped by discussing various points in personal conversations. The list includes Roscoe C. Martin, Robert J. Harris, Richard J. Russell, T. V. Smith, Frederick C. Mosher, Frank Piskor, Stuart Gerry Brown, Milton Williams, Jerome Frank, E. E. Schattschneider, Fowler Harper, Tom Emerson, Leonard D. White, Charles E. Merriam, Harold Stein, Wayne A. R. Leys, and Earle H. Ketcham. Acknowledgment of a more general indebtedness should include Louis Brownlow, Arthur Macmahon, John Gaus, Don K. Price, Pendleton Herring, V. O. Key, Jr., Chester Barnard, Merle Fainsod, Wallace Sayre, Charles McKinley, David Truman, Donald C. Stone, and Herbert Emmerich.

P. H. A.

TABLE OF CONTENTS

I

PRIVATE AND PUBLIC ORGANIZATIONS

MORALITY is a conception deriving from, and developed in, associations of human beings. If it may be said to begin in consideration of others, it does not end there, since an individual who would defer to another individual in all things would invite on the part of the second immoral actions inconsiderate of the first. The self-interest which insists upon one's own dignity as a factor in the association is thus an essential, even if wholly inadequate, criterion of a "good" action.

Morality begins in arrangements between human beings, ordering relationships to mutual advantage but with mutual discipline. Even in the simplest of human associations these arrangements involve the reconciliation of differing values. Negotiation is minimized by establishing these arrangements as habits, customs, taboos, freeing those concerned to come to terms about new problems in new understandings or in amendments to old ones.

Even the simplest of associations involves elements of governance—leadership, determination, execution, enforcement, and responsibility. As associations become more complex and more specialized, they become more highly organized and interrelated. All human organizations are systematic pursuits of various values. In turn, their conduct becomes a more and more important aspect of the pursuit of values. Public organization is a part of the whole organizational complex, differentiated as a systematic pursuit of *public* values. Democratic government is one of the general forms of public organization peculiarly distinguished by its aspiration to impregnate public values with individual and other private values.

At the point of action the problem of morality becomes an organizational problem and hence also a problem in administration. Democracy itself is largely a means for the determination of, and arrival at, values; but the means are capable of many organizational variations, and if "the end pre-exists in the means," the specific organizational forms themselves pose important value problems. So it is, too, with the action means of administration. Consideration of the moral values to be sought in public administration may appropriately begin, therefore, with some reference to the general organizational phenomena of our time and place.

Private Organization

In all nations there are many private associations, though there is a wide difference, as between nations, in the number and character of such forms. Among primitive peoples, intricate and in many ways confining though their relationships are, the number of private associations is relatively small and the variety of activities restricted. Of advanced peoples, none approach us in the United States in number and variety of private associations and activities. These groupings provide altogether vastly more of the patterns and disciplines of life than does government.

How many millions of organizations we have in America, probably no one knows. Even defining "organization" for census terms would be difficult; for example, is a church in Oshkosh an organization or are all of the Methodist churches an organization? Is a Rotary Club in Cedar Rapids an organization or is it merely a part of Rotary International?

According to any definition, however, we must have many millions of organizations of many different kinds with many purposes. Families, churches, businesses, lodges, and clubs alone would make a great total. Functional associations, such as professional societies, farm organizations, labor unions, chambers of commerce, associations of manufacturers, retail merchants, bakers, millers, dairymen, morticians, cattle growers, horticulturists, and candlemakers, contribute important additions. Social, religious, economic, and cultural expressions of common interest take manifold forms. Alexis de Tocqueville, as quoted by Emerson D. Fite in *Government by Co-operation*, testified to the peculiar development of this aspect of the American culture more than a century before the attainment of its present dimensions and variety:

The Americans of all ages, all conditions and all dispositions constantly form associations. They have not only commercial and manufacturing companies in which all take part, but associations of a thousand other kinds, religious, moral, serious, futile, restricted, enormous, or diminutive. The Americans make associations to give entertainments, to found establishments for education, to send missionaries to the antipodes, and in this manner they found hospitals, prisons, schools. . . . Wherever at the head of some new undertaking you see the government in France or a man of rank in England, in the United States you will be sure to find an association.

No doubt this organizational drive is deeply related to a widespread search for identification of self with society, for participation, influence, and dignity. It is a phenomenon related to the division-of-labor principle and to the specialization now come to distinguish modern life. The academic world also both reflects and advances the characteristic; the terms "chemist" and "physicist" are no longer descriptive of specialization, and one must know what subfield of what field of either of those two sciences a particular person occupies to be able to place him in a job or to identify his role in society. We no longer seek a teacher of "political science," but one in "public law" or "theory" or "politics" or "public administration" or—still more specialized—one in "local government" or "state government" or "public personnel" or "public budgeting."

The proliferation of organizations does not end the search for identification of one's place in society. Even though the organizations together provide more status for more persons, and more uniquely identifiable functions and memberships, there are within each organization problems of status, leadership, and differences in influence and rank. The labor union formed to represent certain interests of workers as a group is itself necessarily an organization in which many members may feel themselves and their multiple and different interests inadequately represented. So feeling, they join other associations; from each one they get some means of expression; in each the means are limited by deference to others and the disciplines of the particular organization; in all of the organizations together they obtain something less than full self-expression and derive new values not anticipated.

In all private associations most persons come to realize their own limited personal influences and the greater influence of a few who emerge as leaders. The individual's status, assignments, and rewards are outside his personal control, and his voice seems not to yield much influence in decisions highly important to him. Frustration and the sense of injustice arise, not first or even most often or most importantly with respect to government, but with respect to private associations. The disciplines that bear most heavily upon him are private disciplines. Those of the family and job association are heaviest and most constant, but in every outreaching the restraints and arrangements of the additional associations are encountered.

In the family if the husband assumes headship his wife

cannot fail to ask at least subconsciously, "Why not I?" In the business organization few employees can believe themselves less capable than the associate who was promoted. In organizational membership the questions are many and varied: "Why was I not put on the committee?" "Why was I not consulted?" "Why did 'they' not do as I suggested?" In the great complexity of affairs the remote executive seems always to have acted without knowledge of what the individual employee knew or preferred. Even the executive at the level next up does and must act without knowing all that his subordinates know. In co-operatives, where membership influence has been especially basic, equality of influence has made for poor administration and at times for failure of the enterprise. Sidney and Beatrice Webb, as socialists struggling with this problem, long ago laid down, with reference to only one aspect of it, the dictum that employees of a co-operative even though members should not be permitted to vote on administrative matters. Under the most equal distribution of influence, therefore, effective organization involves concentrations of power and responsibility, and arrangement of these in hierarchies. This is the pattern of bureaucracy, the universal essential to purposeful organization.

Private organization has not been generally expected to have as much democratic character as that required of popular government, though the growth of democratic expectation has not been limited to the field of government. One general result of the democratic impetus has been to heighten administrative concern with human relations and to develop techniques of employee consultation and participation. Another has been the proliferation of organizations representative of tangential interests. Another has been to develop definitely auxiliary or parallel organizations, such as unions, representative of basic employee interests. Still another has been to turn to public opinion and finally to government as mediums for effecting changes in the private field.

Fruits of such developments are on the whole substantial, and their extension and perfection are to be anticipated. Yet at every stage the vehicle chosen—organization—is itself possessed of characteristics similar to those for which amelioration is sought. The pluralizing of organization and the increase in specialization pluralize individuality and complicate the problem of relating the person to society generally, as it complicates the problem of ordering society. New dimensions are given to the task of reconciling individual and group values with organizational and administrative necessities and of relating individuals to organizational activities requiring differentiations in influence and responsibility.

Not all such differentiation is resented, of course. Deference is variously sought, achieved, and yielded. Many employees are so interested in their specialized tasks as to have little desire for hierarchal place. Many recognize no great interest in numerous decisions organizationally made, and often there is a willing, if vague, deference to the organizational necessities and to the leadership associated with hierarchal status. There is even complaint about "too many committees" and "too many conferences," and insistence upon receiving directions and getting on with the work. But in the background there is an enduring concern about the locus of organizational power, the way it is exercised, and differentiations in influence. Without an understanding of these organizational materials of life in which administration and specialized functions are seen as complementary and important to each other, administration is regarded grudgingly as a "necessary evil." Yet only through organization do individuals confer large effectiveness upon each other and upon themselves; it is the vehicle through which social values and individual values alike are advanced, or lost. The individual's management of his organizational memberships is therefore of immeasurable importance to him.

As a separate social being the individual finds expression and wields influence chiefly through organizations and in terms of their products. Areas of private membership—ranging from family to neighborhood, community, church, school, club, employment, professional or business group, and on interminably—are vastly more numerous and greater in total content than zones of public membership in party and governmental jurisdiction. They provide the individual not only the greatest reserve of restraint and discipline but also a stupendous measure of choice for the exercise of discretion, a problem altogether unmanageable for him in its totality but an asset unequaled in any other time and place in history. He can manage his life only by targeting his attention and energies. By inattention he perforce delegates to others his shares in concerns both minimal and vital. In a society so richly complex, perhaps the individual's most pressing need is for facilities which reduce the ranges of his choice to somewhat manageable proportions as, in the public sphere, his choice of presidential possibilities finally is effectively reduced to two. Perhaps there is need in the private scene for techniques which, metaphorically speaking, shorten the long ballot to fit the individual's span of attention and trim his participation to his finitude. Aided by such techniques, and with attention and membership progressively concentrated on his most general and central concerns, he may avoid the frustrations of trying to be more responsible and knowledgeable than reality permits. Only guilt accrues from moral gluttony. Some solace of philosophy he needs, too. Some of this he might acquire by pondering the simple but profound facts that a wide consensus can never be identical with any individual view and that his own opinion of any matter, reached in a state of relative irresponsibility, would not be the same if he were vested—and weighted—with the power of decision.

These problems of membership are significant because the organizational efforts are generally in pursuit of values. Since such private endeavor produces much of the social context of government and many of the materials with which government must deal, it appears desirable to explore briefly some of the important private moralities before turning attention to public organizations and their moral problems.

As already suggested, all organizations build upon individual self-interest in approaching mutuality of interest. Mere assumption of responsibility for one's own survival is translated into responsibility for one's family, and then for group well-being. Individual interest and group interest, while not synonymous, are related in developing foresight, enlightenment, and morality, as all private interests are similarly related to public interest. These are relationships of different values, and often of values in conflict. In an oversimplified way self-interest may be viewed as the first rung in an extensible ladder. For a long time in respect to business, and it alone, this first rung was rationalized into a full-length ladder, the theory being that if all individuals would exert themselves to maximize personal advantage, the total result would be maximum benefit for society. In retrospect it seems a great wonder that this view was so widely held.

The theory of *laissez faire*, like the sequential Marxism, reflects the tendency to either-or formulations found in many efforts to do systematic thinking. It was an effort to be "completely scientific" or "completely logical" contrary to the nature of men. It was an effort to separate moral concerns entirely from the systematic consideration of social action, coming to be anomalously justified in the peculiar moralities of such a system. It applied to only one area of social action, denying to that area the rationality possible under conscious management in favor of the "pure" rationality of a way of regarding it. It applied to the general area of economics a thinking no businessman ever would have applied to the conduct of his own enterprise. It was recognized as absurd to suppose that an entrepeneur would say to potential employees, "Come to work as you wish, and do here whatever appeals to you as in your own interest; there will be no direction of your efforts, no planning; I'm sure that your selfish efforts will be in entire harmony with my self-interest and the self-interest of my company." In practice the mixing of direction and individual discretion in the frame of an established discipline denies in the private, as well as in the public, field the simplification of either-or thinking and keeps open the door to the pursuit of diverse values.

Man's greater capacity for survival, as compared with other species, may turn on his greater capacity for the altruistic. Conscious and extensive appeal to self-interest may minimize this capacity and maximize disorder and brutishness. It was with such concern that Lincoln Steffens in his *Autobiography* presented the fable of Adam, Eve, and the apple in order to identify the fatal apple as capitalism. Steffens was turning, or had turned, to communism.

Certainly the absence of restraint on self-interest in absolute free trade would lead to wholesale robbery, violence, and social chaos. Even with only moderate imposition of restraints, private business in its raw form stimulates sharpness, aggressiveness, ruthlessness. All societies have felt compelled to impose on the pursuit of self-interest restraints so substantial as to nullify the generalization that simple pursuit of self-interest serves to secure social good. Even under such restraints the conflict between imposed and induced social responsibility and the mores of business has often occasioned confusion and frustration. All of us have known small-scale businessmen who have squeezed and gouged quite mercilessly and ingeniously in business, and on Sunday or in civic affairs have given much evidence of benevolence and social concern. Many of them have felt, insofar as they have rationalized their inconsistency, that they have adhered to the morality of business in the one area and to a different morality in the other. Competition thus tends to force ethics as well as prices to the lowest point in the competitive situation. The corporation, too, was in the first instance, as E. A. Ross expressed it, a channel for men's greed and not for their consciences.

But restraints have been imposed in all societies and nations, and in advancing civilizations there has been rather steadily the tendency to increase them. Given fairly substantial beginnings of order, those with commercial inclinations have always been among the first to seek its enlargement, seeing richer opportunities under order than under disorder. Their search has been in part, of course, a simple projection of self-interest in order of their own making under their dominance. It is natural for those in business to seek to limit the effects of competition, to stabilize competitive relationships, to ensure markets and sources of supply, and to monopolize fields small or great. Often, however, when restraints have been imposed for the sake of different and larger interests, these have come to be accepted as reducing the hazards of disorder. New disorder comes into view as society becomes more complicated, and new moral concerns emerge. Sometimes because of public concern and sometimes supported by the march of business interest, the new or newly recognized disorder has been offset by the establishment of new restraints.

Imposition of restraints by the government has been

crucial everywhere, although far from coextensive with this whole pattern. Government enters the scene early to open the way to private restraints upon private pursuit of gain, directly intervenes on occasion, remains always as a special overhanging influence because of its capacity to intervene, and on this account, as Beardsley Ruml has suggested in *Tomorrow's Business*, indirectly effects more restraint on undisciplined self-interest than it actually imposes. No moderately developed society has ever had a free trade susceptible of realistic description in terms of laissez-faire theory, and with all its restraints on trade this country probably approaches that theory more nearly than does the economy of any other similarly advanced nation. Free competition, even as limited as we know it to be in the United States, would never have been so richly beneficial, nor indeed even feasible, had there not been here a watchful government equipped to deal directly with social conditions consequent to it. Noneconomic private associations of diverse sorts—benevolent, social, and cultural—also participate importantly in the achievement, independent of commerce, of equities and other values essential to popular satisfaction.

Altogether, the combined pattern of developed customs, popular expectations, governmental action, and private initiative has been carried to some points where enlightened self-interest and sheer altruism are sometimes indistinguishable. Generally—and particularly for large enterprise—it has resulted in a great multiplication of the objectives and responsibilities of private business. R. A. Gordon reports in *Leadership in Large Corporations* that among principal business executives in this country there is much confusion about the responsibilities of management. He says in effect that while business was once expected rather simply to make maximum profits for stockholders, social exactions now are so numerous and diverse that executives are most uncertain about how to equate them.

The momentum of business in this and other democratic nations is toward steadily rising standards, and under growing governmental and social restraint, toward greatly accelerated production. The Committee for Economic Development, a research-and-education organization of enlightened businessmen, has reported that in terms of the 1949 dollar, earnings per man-hour (the clearest indication of real income presently available for the periods given) increased very substantially more between 1929 and 1939 than ever before in our history and went on to still a higher record in the following decade when wartime controls provided extreme interference for some years. Earnings per man-hour increased fourteen cents (in terms of the 1949 dollar) between 1920 and 1929, twenty-five cents between 1929 and 1939, and thirty-three cents between 1939 and 1949. Of course it does not follow that maximizing governmental controls is a simple formula for further progress. But that capitalism may find its richest and most satisfying development in a moving balance with governmental response to felt public need is clearly suggested by our twentieth-century history. The rising standards of business, associated with unparalleled increases in productivity, reveal beneficent consequences of democratic government, while fascism and communism reveal staggering difficulties of other systems. These things had not begun to be so clear in the days of Steffens.

There were two crucial errors in the ivory-tower logic of Marx. One was his assumption that laissez-faire theory would continue to dominate in capitalist states and that government would inevitably be merely the creature of capitalism. The right to survive has been earned by, con-

ferred upon, and imposed upon, capitalism through its sub-
mission to direct public interference and to the expansion
of government in amelioration of consequences of the
capitalistic system. The considerable elevation of business
practice, seemingly spontaneous, is basically the consequence of these two causes. It may be said, however, that
the two factors have brought about conditions in which
businessmen have been enabled to impregnate business
with more of the idealism which they have in common with
all others.

The second fundamental error of Marx was in his exclusive preoccupation with economics, which leads too
many others to subordinate politics to economics and which
led him to exclude politics and government from his logic.
The inevitable consequences of his unmodified doctrine
have been made clear, since the time of Steffens, in the
Soviet dictatorship. Everywhere today it should be abun-
dantly clearer than ever before that the choice of economic
systems, like other choices, is not between the perfect and
the imperfect, and that in matters economic, as in those governmental, the moral preference is for a system in which
responsibility is to society and public and for a system the
choice of which is a public choice, the conduct of which is
subject to public influence and even to public control. This
subordinates the choice of economic systems to the political
and makes economic policy continuously secondary to political policy. The most significant contrast between the Soviet
Union and the United States is not in their economies but
in their governments. Similarly, the great contrast between
orthodox socialism as confessedly developed in the Soviet
Union and the socialism of the British Labor party has been
the latter's choice of popular, parliamentary, political control.

Our own advance is indicated along a different path, with

relatively little public ownership and much private ownership, but with increasingly social and public-interest objectives guarded over by a government probably more richly
political than any other in the world. Even then, the practices
of private business will be in far from uniform accord with
the standards in those areas where determinations have public
character. As of today public moral standards are hostile to
the self-perpetuating hierarchies of managerial control described by Gordon as characteristic of important private organizations and popularly accepted in them. Great parts of
the pattern of personal pursuit of gain have long been excluded from the public field. Nepotism in business has never
come much under public scrutiny, but its counterpart in
popular government long ago came under severe restriction.
Continuing contracts for purchase from companies closely
associated are one example of a kind of favoritism having
various forms in business and increasingly excluded from the
public field. For business, even the special kind of popular
character which would take the form of stockholder control
has slight reality. Private affairs are exposed to no important
fractional part of the jealous scrutiny given to government;
standards and procedures are correspondingly and pervasively different.

Private institutions do reflect and contribute to changing
conditions and are in varying ways more or less responsive
to changing expectations of their memberships. But only recently have most of them come to be considered much in
terms of a "political" structure and function. None of the
more important organizations are nearly so consciously or
systematically patterned to make for responsiveness as are
public, democratic institutions. Even if they were so designed, the results would not be the same as public responsiveness; membership in any private association is less than
"the public" soon to be defined, and membership in all priv-

ate associations altogether does not constitute the public. Nor would complete democratization of all private organizations create a democratic state or resolve its manifold problems; the great task of relating them to each other and to them as a whole in terms of values different from their separate ones still would remain.

It is true, too, that many private group operations constitute extremely slight translations of harsh and narrow selfish interest into something more broadly social. Very often their social justification is in little besides a fuzzy claim to participation in the function of producing economic goods or services; this is a cloak that may, and often does, cover quacks, charlatans, procurers, and ruthless exploiters. In the entire sales field there is an unsystematic but fairly general reliance for the fixing of standards on a process which may be regarded as part of the politics of business. Whatever may be sold is on that account justified as demonstrating the meeting of a social need. The market for any single company is almost always a minority market, of course, and very often the search for mass sales is an effort to find the lowest common denominator of standards held by the largest available minority. It is a curious fact that many who criticize government in its search for majority support themselves find social justification in their appeals to minority mass markets. The whole system is one which produces many important goods and many trivia, considerable improvement in daily living and not inconsiderable pandering to the vicious, with wastes of many kinds not much taken into account.

Some business practices in ways not often considered discriminate against the poor. One recalls, for example, the concern of an unusually discerning and responsible merchant in one small town whose trade was with the poor in a situation giving him intimate acquaintance with them. "They buy shoes of the poorest quality and lowest price because they never have enough money to pay for better ones, but in the course of a year they spend more for shoes than persons in better circumstances," he said. In realization of the problem, this merchant so reduced his own margins that in a few years he went into bankruptcy! Business practice has been author of the saying that those who have get. Its raw logic is to treat ability to buy and ability to invest as simple and final indexes of merit.

William G. Sheppard wrote for *Collier's* in the twenties a series of articles entitled "Too Many Retailers," making the point a man in the oil business once made briefly in conversation by saying, "If I should start in my car at Richmond to drive to Los Angeles, buying a pint of gasoline at each filling station I passed, when I arrived at Los Angeles I should have not only a full tank in my car but two full tank-trucks besides." The high rate of business failures is therefore an important item of cost in the system of free competition. At the other end of the business scale, some of the strongest concerns find their strength, not in economic precision, but in some priority of position, momentum, and superior resources capable of eliminating competition or in the early possession of some crucial patents.*

The purpose here, however, is not to attempt an over-all evaluation of private business but to suggest terms of scrutiny contributing to a thoughtful consideration of the entire organizational scene, private and public. While it is true that a comparison of the per capita income in the United States with per capita income in Haiti has little precise meaning because only an unknown portion of the differ-

---

* For various related discussions see: Karl W. Kapp, *Social Costs of Private Enterprise* (Cambridge, 1950); H. A. Overstreet, *The Mature Mind* (New York, 1949); and Reinhold Niebuhr, *Children of Light and Children of Darkness* (New York, 1945).

ence favorable to the United States is reflected in intrinsics, the rest being chargeable to waste, taste, style, and the great overhead involved in achieving that difference, it also is true that the development of the economy in the United States is in net very substantially higher than anywhere else in the world. This fact does give general testimony to the service of our system, even if it does not justify the sentimental, wholesale, and uncritical extravagance of some of its defenders.

It might be supposed that the rate of economic expansion would slacken as the attainment of necessities approaches the universal in a society. But the popular view of what is necessary grows with new attainment, and there is now recognized a clear dynamism in science and technology. It is true, however, that there is a gradual shift to a proportionately greater output of services, in contrast with the production of raw materials and fabricated goods, and that the provision of services is ever more important to the raising of the standard of living. Some of these services are an expansion of profit-system efforts, ranging from the transference of weaving and soapmaking from the household to the market place, through the dry-cleaning and window-washing ventures, and on to the rather curious offices that undertake to fill any and all calls for help. Health services of the regular commercial sort, vacation resorts, guide services, etc., further illustrate the trend.

Private organizations of a nonprofit sort are also important in the service field, however, especially if service be loosely defined. The churches themselves and their auxiliary organizations, country clubs, hunting clubs, lodges, volunteer fire departments, hospital associations, co-operatives, endowed schools and colleges, and historical associations are illustrative. Many interest groups, such as farm organizations, unions, and chambers of commerce, also provide services somewhat apart from their agitational functions. The amount of time, personnel, and resources involved in areas outside of the zone of economic competition is extremely large. There is increasing realization of need for services not likely to be met by commercial efforts or not likely to be met in terms of modern expectations. Provision for them is increasingly expected, either through non-profit private organizations or through public action.

A visit to a typical county-seat midwestern town of three thousand or so residents will reveal a surprising number of the more monumental features of that community as developed apart from the conventional commercial incentive: the schools, hospital, airport, park, waterworks, sewage-disposal plant, streets, courthouse, churches and parsonages, Masonic Temple, Knights of Columbus clubhouse, country club, city hall, fire stations, library, civic auditorium, and cemetery. Some of these and like establishments increasingly house services important to modern living standards.

PUBLIC ORGANIZATION

Before the formation of the United States, religious and religiously sponsored establishments among those enumerated in the preceding paragraph were activities of government. The separation of church and state here has transferred such matters from the public to the private zone. Wholly new projects and others once private have become public, as the same list suggests.

John Dewey has given us a profound and useful, even though inadequate, distinction in describing the public as *composed of those indirectly affected by actions done privately* by individuals or intermediate associations. Under his theory those engaged in private associations might be left to handle their own affairs so long as the consequences were restricted to the participants; when persons not directly

taking part become concerned because of indirect consequences of these private actions, then a public comes into
being. However oversimplified this view, it does point
shrewdly to a unique role for government as the agent of
a public or publics so constituted, and it reveals government to be an important and integral part of the whole
organizational complex. It brings into relief the peculiarly
differentiated concerns of government and its moral obligations, revealing the inanity of affirmations that private
organizations are inherently good and government inherently bad or at best a "necessary evil." Such statements
would decree evil for the larger organ of civilization, denying humanity as a whole a vehicle for the pursuit of good.

At least a minimum of variety in organizational forms,
in relationship to each other, is essential to a sufficient
expression of human concerns. If only unions of workers
existed, management would have to be invented; when
business organization was restricted to its managerial-
hierarchal form, the complementary forming of unions
was found to be necessary. Private organizations similarly
call for public organization as their complement; if only
government existed, private organization would be required to enrich and diversify means of human activity and
aspiration. Conflicts of interests—differences in values—exist within all organizational forms and between them, conflicts between individual member and the whole organization, conflicts between subgroups and between individuals
and subgroups. Such conflicts are implicit in organizations,
and the organizations are at the same time means for achieving workable harmony. There is nothing peculiar about
government-citizen relationships in this respect. Government is peculiar in its role in the organizational whole, as
unions are peculiar, as management is peculiar, as churches
are peculiar. A good many of the different organizations

are clearly necessary complements to each other. Concern for the ethical values to be pursued through government must be related to this whole societal picture. The special roles of government, its peculiar nature, and alternative forms and processes are basic elements in our judgments of its value judgments.

Reaffirming the importance of Dewey's distinction, we need to consider its possible incompleteness as an identification of the nature of a public and its concerns. If we accept Chester Barnard's definition of an organization as including its customers, it is plain that in many nations publics have called upon government to act with respect to problems arising wholly within private organizations. The regulation of railroads and other utilities was demanded by their customers. Stock-exchange regulation, for which agitation was growing among members, was actually imposed, on the other hand, because of public realization of the essentially public consequences of exchange activities. Industrial employees are surely to be classified as members of their organizations; even before the industrial revolution had got well under way they turned to government to act in behalf of their special concerns as members. The principal source of demands for tariffs has been the producers seeking protection of their private interests. The Dairy Bureau of the United States Department of Agriculture owes its existence to the influence of dairy farmers seeking private benefits. Public provision of certain traffic policemen has been made in behalf of transit companies, those special officers often expediting the movement of streetcars at the expense of other traffic.

Many other government services valuable to citizens generally may not have been provided in realization of indirect consequences of private activities but in aid of such activities. A public that comes into being in recognition of indirect consequences of private activities would usually be concerned about correcting—in public terms—the activities having the indirect consequences. Not to reform but to expedite private business, in the first instance at least, government has instituted monetary systems. For much the same reason it has built roads and conducted weather, statistical, and research services. The most important of foreign-policy problems may not originate in private transactions within a particular state, but wholly outside its borders, and perhaps in public action outside its borders. Foreign policy may be said to have begun in part as an insurance of continuity for domestic private affairs and in part as the not unrelated business of saving the government itself.

No matter how much we might question particular governmental actions in their behalf, we could not seriously contend that government must be excluded from action largely conceived as in aid of private interests. Nor could we deny the right and duty of government to defend itself and to deal with other sovereign governments. Expanding Dewey's dictum, then, we may say that a public comes into being in recognition of some need, for the meeting of which there seems—to those constituting the public—to be no satisfactory private means. If the need is widely felt or influentially expressed, the result is to pose a public issue and perhaps to secure public action. Serving private activities, preserving the government as an agency of private associations and publics, dealing with the indirect consequences of private transactions, and actions in which these elements are combined provide the roles of government. Services most generally useful in private affairs are, of course, not too sharply separable from actions dealing with indirect consequences of private transactions, and the preservation of government would be auxiliary to those two functions. It may be, therefore, that we have explained rather than modified Dewey's dictum. And surely his distinction is worthy of enduring emphasis as pointing clearly to a role available only to government. A private organization attempting to deal with the indirect consequences of private transactions would become a public organization and assume the role of governance.

So explained, the dictum sets up no definite limits for government; only the public does that, in successive determinations. This would appear to be true for any government, although the size, character, and facilities of the public differ widely among states. Bismarck's definition of politics as "the art of the possible" testifies to his understanding that the public ultimately sets governmental limits, and Bismarck was not exactly a full-blown democrat nor was he speaking with reference to achieved democracy. Evaluation of a particular government, its forms, processes, and specific actions, then, would relate to one's judgment of the wisdom of a particular public or the membership of that public, the political processes by which public judgment is developed and expressed, and the administrative processes by which the judgment is translated into governmental action. It must be appraised, in other words, in terms of organizational structure and performance and in its context, a very large part of which is private.

Some ethical questions concerning government are identical with those concerning private associations. Personal gain at the expense of a partnership with which one is affiliated, embezzlement or theft of any kind, lying, and hypocrisy, as hostile to confident co-operation in private association, are evils equally to be avoided in public work. Personal venality in ordinary terms, when it is discovered within the government, is not in any way peculiar to government and therefore requires little treatment in these pages. Here the search is for ethical concerns differentiated from private ethical concerns, whether by being heightened or by having marked dissimilarity related to the special role of government or to the special character sought in a particular scheme of government.

All governments, for example, are generally held to be distinguished by the possession and exercise of peculiarly coercive powers. It is true, of course, that government everywhere, desirably as well as necessarily, is vested with certain overriding powers over private powers and that these may not be wisely limited in many specific and formal ways so as to remove the overhanging potential. In the view of the individual, private associations also produce effects similar to, and suggestive of, those inherent in overriding powers, and the existence of government provides him a theoretical choice between these private powers and public powers. How real his choice may be is an ethical question of central importance. Who is the agent exercising an overriding power? How is the agent responsible? How limited in fact and how controlled? These are questions related to fundamental human values as they are involved in all organizational performance. Private powers may be the more easily tolerated in the knowledge that certain recourse may be had to government. Private powers may be permitted to be less responsible to members, less controllable by members so long as members have knowledge of the possibility of actual appeal to government.

Probably no organization has ever exercised nearly all of the powers theoretically available to it, and power potential is therefore a factor somewhat separable from the actual exercise of power. If governmental power is insufficiently used in response to the public sense of need—if appeal to government is difficult and ineffective—stresses accumulate and conditions invite explosive and extreme expressions of public power. If appeal to government is easy, it will be less necessary and less used in conditions otherwise the same. This is true because of accelerated private response to social expectations, stimulated by realization of the ability of the public to utilize government for intervention. The more widely available the facility of popular appeal to government is, the less coercive the exercise of governmental powers tends to be.

In a nation of great popular character, its social scene distinguished by innumerable and varied private organizations, a good many of which constitute huge vestings of private power, heavily charged fields of force are set up. Much of the complex play of force is unintended, much of it unmanageable by those who in coming together generate it. The whole field creates conditions for which no private group is particularly or especially responsible. Government inevitably emerges in dimensions commensurate to the context as the agency of coherence and balance. Whatever its specific activities, government's fundamental role is unique, basically different from all private roles. The performance of government may be properly appraised only in terms appropriate to the whole organizational complex of which it is a part. But concern with morality in its processes must relate chiefly to its differentiated role.

II

GOVERNMENT AND MORALITY

THE quality of government cannot properly be appraised if it is not sufficiently realized that government is, first and last, an organization—undisputed heir to the strengths and weaknesses associated with disciplined and systematic group performance. It must be similarly realized that the conduct of government is inevitably and intricately related to the pattern of private organization within, and to the patterns of public organization without, its boundaries. Governments differ among themselves, and each one undergoes change, in large part because of various and changing private organizational patterns. They differ further within the wide limits set by organizational necessity. The differences reflect and embody efforts in pursuit of different value conceptions.

Governmental value questions vary widely in generality, specificity, form, and application and in the degree to which they are regarded as means values or as end values. Democracy is distinguished by, among other differentiations, the high reliance it places on the means values of governmental forms and processes. In this respect it is in sharpest and frankest contrast with communism. Lenin's advice to the Communist party of Russia to "resort to all sorts of devices, maneuvers and illegal methods, to evasion and subterfuge" applied not only to efforts before Communist ascendancy, it reflected a general belief, now clearly characteristic of Soviet practice at home as well as abroad, that the end justifies the means. Communism thus bypasses multitudinous and varied value problems which are of constant concern in the conduct of democratic government.

The present discussion of American public administration considers value involvements of the means by which executive government participates in the continuing business of realizing democracy.

DEMOCRATIC GOVERNMENT

Democratic government is no less than any other government involved in the function of governance, and it therefore requires no less the vesting of an overriding power potential, which no less involves disciplines. The democratic ideology is not anarchic; rather, it is a scheme for the impregnation of government with special popular values which leave open the way to popular determination of other values.

The general theory of democracy, before it is developed into more specific theory of the conduct of its business, calls simply for a state whose people are empowered to make and unmake its government, with freedom of opinion and expression and with equality as citizens. These are the ingredients of the ideal of *political* freedom, but the ideal is only to be realized in the continuing operation of government dedicated to it and at the same time performing its regular and complicated business of governance. The general theory is widely accepted and fairly well understood in its general terms, but there seems to be no adequately comprehensible theory of its application and its relation to the business of governance. The notion of freedom is thinly extended into a vague anarchism in which there is expectation that governmental discipline will be absent. The notion of democracy is treated in individual rather than in organizationally functional terms, separating the citizen emotionally and intellectually from consistent identification with the popular instrument.

From time immemorial philosophers have realized that freedom is to be achieved only through the disciplines of organization. This has been special knowledge, however, somehow not widely available, alien even to great numbers of the highly cultivated whose specialized learning has been in fields remote from political philosophy. Indeed, specialization of education and subsequent concentration in isolated fields—made possible only by complex organization of education and human business—result in the highest differentiation, and hence individualization, of men ever attained, and their individualism turns generally resentful of the organizational performances that created them. Many of them are leaders in the antigovernment school, unconsciously at least making reputable for the less learned their own misunderstanding. Often they are among those who grudgingly defer to government as at best a "necessary evil."

Just so, some may regard sex as a necessary evil, or the time required to eat as unwonted diversion of energies from things intrinsically more important. Yet in such a quixotic view, life is predestined at last to make sense only to cynics, and freedom to be lost. All the characteristics of finite men and their physical universe are the materials of life, and it is real life in which values are to be found and developed. Value approaches maturity only in forms associative, and government is a universal necessity in advancing human association. Freedom is a product of organization, and so is discipline. For the highly individualistic self-expression possible through music one must master the disciplines of music. Similarly, for self-realization in social affairs there must be use of the discipline of organizational action. Within these disciplines alone can freedom be achieved.

Democratic government has to do first of all only with political freedom and its disciplines; the totality of freedom is dependent upon private associations and their freedoms and upon the totality of public and private organizations. The right to have membership in private associations, and to choose among them, is an important part of the whole condition; freedom is found within and among all the elements in the associative complex. Democratic government is distinguished by special recognition of this fact. It is designed in moral concern as an improved form and method of governance. It is intended to provide a readier vehicle for a wider public, which consequently will act with fuller regard for values individually and in associations private, striving for a different kind of balance in these values. It does not escape or automatically solve the hard problems of common concern; it treats them in different terms.

Philosophers are not wise enough to tell us what particular decisions to make in the conduct of social business. The problems they set out to solve are intellectual and abstract, not the specific problems faced by social operators. Their solutions, even appropriately general and speculative, still are often in terms antecedent to the highly complicated texture of modern practice and therefore difficult to relate to present reality. Made as full-bodied as possible, their formulations still would be designed to illumine the field of action, not to relieve its captains of their responsibilities. At a lower level of abstraction, our present effort is to spotlight particular segments of the action field.

We therefore beg the more general questions which philosophers ruminate; we begin by assuming democracy. The assumption leaves room for those who believe that the good derives directly from deity, unless they insist upon the fixation of political authority in specific centers of revelation. Dogma only damns the differences we must honor. Here it is assumed that the separation of church and state, resulting in plural churches, advances democracy and that in democracy the divinely good comes to bear upon affairs through the influence of human beings diversely sensitive and differentially responsive. Pluralism is both the presupposition and the precipitate of democracy.

The assumption similarly leaves room for those who differ about many other basically philosophical conceptions. It does not entirely bypass, however, some of the general moral arguments peculiarly posed by "democracy," "majority government," the "public will," the "public interest," and the process of compromise in operations of public concern. As we relate these terms to governmental action it is desirable to give them some definition indicative of their limitations as precise ideas or guides.

It is no admission of an unavoidably evil character for democratic government to see it as merely preferable in a field of other possibilities. The pursuit of moral action is everywhere—not in government alone—carried on through exercise of preference. Democracy is a preference for popular government as contrasted with a concentration of governmental prerogatives in some special class. Reliance generally on majority determination is similarly a preference for the majority as contrasted with a minority and for a simple majority as contrasted with less feasible agreements approaching unanimity.

Fear of democracy is often couched in terms of a possible "tyranny of the majority." Here the choice of democracy is dictated by a greater fear of tyranny at the hands of a minority and by the confidence borne out by experience that search for a majority in practice defers greatly to minorities.

A majority is fluid, usually made up of minorities and capable of rebuilding by appeal to other minorities.

Some of the fear of the majority has been a fear held by the privileged minority, notably the economically privileged, and indeed some of the substance of what they fear is promised in the theory of democracy. Some of this fear is expressed today in affirmations that "too many are being given too much education." Insofar as this particular form of the fear of the majority is concerned, those other than the inordinately privileged may find it justified perhaps only in New Zealand. There, outside of the basic political field, the equalitarian drive which is somewhat implicit in the democratic ideal has been carried to a point so diminishing incentives to excellence as to damage social dynamics. Experience there must be admitted to point toward a real, if for most of the world far from imminent, danger. It is not to be imagined that democracy is absolutely without dangers, but on the other hand it should not be doubted that the danger of equalitarian excess can be well met. So far as the United States is concerned, privilege more than equalitarianism threatens dynamism; this nation and the Soviet Union share honors for first rank in disparity of income. In all nations, more conscious and systematic dealing with incentive in its conventional sense and with incentive as subsidy should be directed toward reconciling and maximizing both equity and dynamics.

In a profounder way the fear of the majority has been fear of "absolute democracy," to use Edmund Burke's phrase. In this has been a particular concern for "the better class of citizens" less in terms of their privilege than in terms of their special capacities. This concern about leadership and general use of "better minds" has often foreseen the greatest advantage in some combination form of government in which the democratic factor has had some function of review and veto and in which another factor has been some kind of open-end group flexibly and responsibly constituting a sort of governing class. In our own nation the same kind of concern has been reflected in insistence upon "representative" or "republican" government in partial contrast with "democratic" government.

In practice large and complicated states appear unable to approach absolute democracy and inevitably have much of the representative character and many of the checks on popular determinations which some see as valuable and some as blemishes. In these pages the emphasis upon organizational performance is a way of side-stepping the republican-democratic dichotomy in pointing to inevitable differences in functions and responsibilities and to the utility of leadership. The impact of science and the general advance of civilization produce a complexity which both requires and induces extensive governmental use of the expert and the generally cultivated. A principal value problem is in keeping this development sufficiently tied to popular control. A second principal problem of related significance lies in the difficulty of establishing majorities in the United States and the consequent threat of tyrannous minority interests with the regression of many decisions from the area open to effective public control. Certainly our record is so heavily one of inconsistent governmental actions—some of it warranted as a proper product of pluralism and some resulting from an excessive dictation by minority interests—that it points sharply away from a tyranny of the majority. This discussion assumes an inevitably representative character in democracy and assumes the reality of democracy to exist in a capacity for popular-majority control, not in the invariable and precise exercise of that control.

For those who accept such assumptions there often remains an unhappiness over an apparent moral loss involved in the process of compromise. By compromise we establish particular democratic institutions; by compromise under democratic institutions we establish majority positions; by compromise under majority positions we carry on governmental actions of diverse sorts in diverse applications. Hence, treating only the subject of administration, we still face the question first raised in theoretical discussion of basic governmental forms. This question inheres in the fact that any compromise seems to those who participate in it to involve a retreat from high ground to lower ground.

This is always a relative question, and often the appearance of retreat is only a matter of point of view. The movement may be a shift in gaze from blue sky to terra firma, a shift from individual concern to common concern, from individual judgment to public decision. Often the sense of loss is associated with the thought, "If *I* had the power to decide, a better decision would be given." Our assumption, to the contrary, is that on the whole in social affairs a decision by *us* is preferable to a decision by *me* and that in public affairs a decision by the public or by public agents is at least in the long run preferable to a private decision. In many respects the objection to compromise is objection to yielding to the social or the public; it is often parochial and may easily support the authoritarian. At the best it is utopianism; at the worst, egoism. The unyielding critic of the compromise essential to harmonious and satisfactory social agreement resembles the mother of the rookie whose comment on the marching troop was, "They're all out of step but my Johnny."

T. V. Smith illumines this problem by discussing the "surplusage of ideals." Everyman, he says, has ideals to which he cannot conform in his every action, some to which he can only vaguely aspire; as he elevates his practice, new insights extend his view of the ideal, and the surplusage not only fails to diminish but on the whole grows faster than utilization. Everyman's practice is, in effect, at the level of his individual compromises. At any given point it represents the highest practicing attainment he there demonstrates capacity to achieve, the surplusage of ideals remaining to light his way to higher ground further on.

Everyman can ask no more of society or public than that they find the highest ground open to their agreement. His judgment of what is the highest ground cannot be their judgment. For individual, group, and public the question is not simply, How far short is this of the ideal? It is equally, Is this higher than before? It is even more, Is this as high ground as we can hope to occupy? For the group, the only meaningful answer is from the group. For the public, the only meaningful answer is from the public; the question is put and the answer given, through the processes of politics. No body of "guardians," no syndicalist expert authority, no Fuehrer, no Quiz Kid can do so well by public criteria— no matter how confident they may be of their own moral competence.

Moral qualms attach stubbornly, however, to reliance upon "the public will." To some the phrase has an unattractive mystical content quite unlike its earthy derivation. To some it indicates a mechanistic, automatic product of a parallelogram of forces not responsive to ideal and spiritual elements; or in psychological terms, it is behavioristic and uninspired by moral quality. But such views are associated with particular notions about human beings and group behavior, and for those who hold such views there is no gain in public morality by changing the pattern of public organization. Reliance on the public will is rich in moral satisfaction for those who see moral capacity in the insights of men both following and leading, and who recognize that the properly moral measure of public leadership is a public measurement.

The public will is flexible and ever subject to change, learning by its own action and by its own experience, so shot through with discretion that it cannot be predicted as though automatic. It is subject to influence by leaders but is capable of discarding leaders. It is energized just as everyman is, by trial and error that is its own, capable of highly enlightened self-interest, capable of devoted altruism, prone to error and given to profiting from and correcting its own mistakes. It is not inherently and invariably right; perhaps it is never right except in its own time and terms. It is not the sum total of all the private wills. It is not even the total of all the private wills after canceling out the pluses and minuses of those wills. It is not distilled in a simple, definite, mechanical way, easy to see and easy to weigh in some merely mechanical weighing machine. It is not to be expressed in terms of some near absolute that leaves no questions to be answered; rather, it is eternally inquisitive. It becomes definite only as a majority will, and since there are many possible majorities, it does not uniformly derive from a particular majority and is not something fixed. It is often expressed only as consent and at times only as a veto. In many instances it is a thing not developed at all, withheld, even nonexistent.

While it is a primary function of politics to achieve agreement of consent in a course of action of common concern, it is another to make agreement unnecessary—to make a public will unnecessary. For the United States to achieve separation of church and state required novel institutional arrangements making agreement about religion unnecessary. There are many ways in which public agreement is avoided. The large delegation to the great area of private association is one. The great and insufficiently recognized achievement of a large area of the personally private is another. Others are provisions for orderly dissent, the governmental doing of inconsistent things in balanced responses to inconsistent demands, and simple failure to agree. (It would be illuminating to review our history to observe how many issues have flared hotly for a time without ever being directly resolved.) Separation of government into levels is another device, promoting variety at least, in agreements achieved. Flexibility and considerateness in the application of law and program also qualify and minimize the business of agreeing.

The public will, then, is a force, largely potential, definite only as majorities form, but always subject to influence of members and leaders. Its capacity to be, more than its being, is the crux of democratic reality. This capacity penetrates the reality of American government.

The public interest is a related phrase of similar character. In a general way it surely is related to concern with consequences of private-association actions beyond the confines of the association. It is also related to concerns wholly outside the private field such as political freedom, foreign policy, and national defense. These two kinds of interest are tempered and modified by a third—regard for private concerns. From this enumeration it should be clear that the public interest is never merely the sum of all private interests nor the sum remaining after canceling out their various pluses and minuses. It is not wholly separate from private interests, and it derives from citizens with many private interests; but it is something distinctive that arises within, among, apart from, and above private interests, focusing in government some of the most elevated aspiration and deepest devotion of which human beings are capable.

More specific determination of the public interest is subject to the public will, but development of alternative concepts of it in changing contexts and applications is especially a responsibility of leadership acting under public influences. The responsibility in one notable part is to take the long view not initially available to the public and to support the long-run good in preference to the short-run advantage. In another part it is to give form and emphasis to interests distinctly public when even in the short view they are different from, or in conflict with, private interests. These responsibilities pose highly complicated problems, but the difficulties are enhanced by a conception of the public interest as involving a heavy obligation to nurture the pluralistic private interests—usually even including those which give rise to the public concern.

DEMOCRATIC MORALITY

Government action, under these assumptions, has basic moral character when it meets certain crucial requirements, no matter how much it may otherwise fall short of satisfying the ideals or interests of single or factional citizens. These basic requirements include the following: that the action conforms to the processes and symbols thus far developed for the general protection of political freedom as the agent of more general freedom; that it leaves open the way for modification or reversal by public determination; that it is taken within a hierarchy of controls in which responsibility for the action may be readily identified by the public; that it embodies as contributions of leadership the concrete structuring of response to popularly felt needs, and not merely responses to the private or personal needs of leaders. These are general elements of a distinctly democratic morality. Their realization is dependent upon detailed processes and arrangements. The details must provide both system and flexibility, both impersonality and magnanimity, authoritative action but action reviewable and open to scrutiny and criticism.

At this more detailed level are the particular political arrangements for popular participation, review and control, political and governmental arrangements for identifying responsibility, and all the processes symbolizing and pursuing fair dealing. Political arrangements may be in fact more or less popular. The locus of responsibility may be unnecessarily clouded. In arrangements and procedures various of the agreed-upon values come in conflict. Here the need for dependable expectations with respect to government may conflict with the need for magnanimity. Here new or newly recognized public needs may be frustrated under familiar procedures, and what was thought to be due process may emerge as a special resource of established privilege. System will point away from whimsy and favoritism, but it may point to the letter and away from the spirit.

Public morality is further complicated by inevitable involvement in private affairs, conceived in different moral terms. Dealing with suppliers, government will both reflect and support the going practices of business, its patronage tending to make big companies bigger. Consultation between government scientists and industrial scientists concerning government research similarly tends to enhance the ability of the large company to profit quickly from developments in the government's laboratories. The close working relationship of officials and citizens is sometimes like the association of two private concerns; often it combines a mixture of such association with a measure of distinctly public-private dealing; and sometimes it becomes a sharply differentiated public-private relationship. Both citizens and officials easily become confused in such a sequence and may fail to identify the peculiarly public values.

Some private moralities having area character complicate the responsibilities of government. Persons in private associations have common reliances and dependence upon, and competitions concerning, area physiography. The differences in natural resources and climate as between regions are associated with differences in economic interests and are marked also by differences in custom. The problem of race relations is first of all a private problem, with areal differentiations. It is a problem dealt with in private associations, as latterly in college fraternities, and it is a problem encountered also by legislatures, courts, and public administrative agencies. At the level of the Department of Justice and the Supreme Court, administrative discretion has been exercised in particular applications of the Fourteenth and Fifteenth amendments ever since their adoption. The most recent decisions of the Court would have been as cogent legally sixty years ago as now, but not equally cogent politically. The result of public practice has been to keep the South under continuing pressure from outside the South, but not at any time fully to impose upon the South a preponderantly outside view. Different results in successive periods have remained somewhere midway between the moving public sentiments in the different areas. This is roughly characteristic of much public administration and similarly characteristic of majority government.

Turning to religious and especially ethical associations of various sorts, we observe not only churches but schools of thought privately determining much of the moral climate for government. Private competition in this field extends across the ideological board, from Puritanism to libertarianism, from egocentric ethics to ethics of universal brotherhood. Because of such private sentiments, we see the numbers racket outlawed in this country although legalized in Germany, slot machines an administrative headache almost everywhere in America although legalized in some jurisdictions and outlawed in others. Similarly, with family life essentially private, we find it almost everywhere a public concern requiring official certification and public control of divorce; some of us see a "bad" national situation in a lack of uniformity in divorce laws, while others see a "good" situation in differential state determination. Private education and private attitudes toward education pose problems conditioning government as the public develops concern for equality of educational opportunity.

While public morality thus in part reflects, incorporates, and is influenced by, private moralities, in another aspect it is sharply distinguished from, and in slight or great conflict with, private values. The function of preserving and developing political freedom is distinctly public, as its values are distinctly public. It has extensive repercussions in private areas. The logic of political equality further supports the emergence of public concerns looking toward equality of opportunity in other than political areas. Political freedom and private freedom produce together a democratic government distinguished by great deference to private interests. One of the fruits of their combined logic is an individualized conception of general welfare gradually become a public concern for the private welfare of individual citizens. Yet we are far from being a welfare state. If foreign affairs, wars, and their aftermath are seen as responsibilities of the government to preserve and develop political freedom within its own boundaries, three fourths of the dimensions and cost of our existing national government are concerned only with that one function.

Even so, with respect to this basic task much remains to be done. While in any nation the effective public is always less than the whole public, many millions of American citizens still are unnecessarily disfranchised or otherwise de-

prived of potentially somewhat equal influence in one way
or another: those in one-party states or in one-party local
jurisdictions; those in whose way special impediments such
as the poll tax are imposed; those in gerrymandered districts;
those in areas where reapportionment of representatives lags
long behind population changes; those in states such as
Georgia where voting arrangements make likely a minority
victory; those faced with too long and confusing ballots;
those whose officials operate under responsibilities not sufficiently open to public identification; those who habitually
refrain from party activity; and those many who live in local
jurisdictions where one party or another is largely the private
property of a powerful clique.

In discussing public administration, however, we bypass
the question of how popular the public is altogether in the
United States or in its various jurisdictions. Accepting the
effective public as it is, the moral problems of the administrator are in his need to balance whole public and private
values and to do this through organizational forms and in
systematic procedures generalized and personal, consistent
and yet flexibly responsive to changing needs and sentiments. Most of all his concern must be with his distinctly
public responsibilities.

He and his colleagues can contribute to the identification
and better organization of the public and can support and
develop means whereby the public may be assured of the
power to judge whether governmental standards are public
standards; they may formulate more truly public standards.
Following the line of least resistance will serve the private,
not the public, interest.

The limitations and necessities of complex organizational
performance are inevitably—and to a considerable degree
happily—barriers to the "absolute" democracy which might
be feared. This is a way of saying that the "bureaucracy"

decried by private interests leans heavily, because of its nature, toward private interests. Individual dissatisfactions with the intricacies of responsible co-ordination, and individual preoccupation with special functions, combine with the total strength in private organizations and the general vogue of hostility to government to give our politics an extraordinarily private color. This inevitably influences actions within public bureaucracies. The public is certainly too little organized; private interests perhaps too much. A chief difficulty in public administration as in politics is to identify the public and to signalize its interest.

With this concern, John Dewey has long since identified two characteristics of our present condition. In *The Public and Its Problems* he spoke first of inadequately flexible institutions:

Industry and inventions in technology, for example, create means which alter the modes of associated behavior and which radically change the quantity, character, and place of impact of their indirect consequences. . . . These changes are extrinsic to political forms which, once established, persist of their own momentum. The new public which is generated remains long inchoate, unorganized, because it cannot use inherited political agencies. . . . To form itself, the public has to break existing political forms. This is hard to do because these forms are the regular means of instituting change. . . . This is why the change of form of states is so often effected only by revolution. The creation of adequately flexible and responsive political machinery has so far been beyond the wit of man.

Dewey might appropriately have noted in this connection that the revolutionary method is not only tragic and wasteful but perhaps usually unsuccessful with respect to its intrinsic objectives. The American Revolution was one of the few in history which projected into early, orderly, and continuing operations the essential aspirations of the revolutionists.

Of the inadequate organization of the public, he said: "There is too much public, a public too diffused and scattered, and too intricate in composition. And there are too many publics, for conjoint actions which have indirect, serious and enduring consequences are multitudinous beyond comparison, and each one of them crosses the others and generates its own group of persons especially affected with little to hold these different publics together in an integrated whole."

Actually government represents and responds to the private associations and not merely to the public indirectly affected by them. Lawyers as an especially potent professional group primarily serve the interests of private associations, not the public cause. In a multiple-organizational society with technologies favorable to the establishment of very large organizations, government is very likely to serve private organizations more and to serve the general, indirectly affected public less.

There is no exclusive responsibility or capacity in public administrators for the meeting of these difficulties. On the contrary, public administration may inadvertently aggravate them. And it may, by conscious effort, help to contain them. The effort requires as much clarification as possible of the differences between private and public morality, and emphasis upon practices and arrangements most in support of the moralities uniquely and critically public.

In many respects, if not in all, it should be plain that public morality is of a higher order than private morality. While private associations represent a translation of individual self-interest into a group concern, the public association represents a higher translation of group interest into public concern. The strictly individual self-interest which would violate a criminal law, similarly yields to the discipline of public punishment. These statements point to much long-established practice which subjects individual and private-group goods to larger, public goods.

The first qualifications to such simplification of moralities are in the democratic insistence upon political freedom. Those individual values which relate to civil liberties and political dynamics are subject to only slight restraints in the name of public order. Freedom of speech and mind are related to the kind of political order desired, in which other individual and private interests are subjected to the possibility of public restraint. Wide room is left here for ranging individual values. The only constitutional exception in the field of private *organizations*, however, outside the political area and in terms other than those of process, is the organization of religion. Religious values are peculiarly related to the personal values largely sheltered by civil liberties. Add to these formal restraints upon the public the public's own expectation of the penetration of governmental action by a magnanimous spirit and we have the principal body of qualifications on the moral priority accorded to the public *capacity* to elevate public considerations over private. The practice is to recognize this priority when the nature of the interests involved is clear.

It is suggested that clarity of this sort develops most readily when public concerns least resemble private concerns. National defense, for example, or foreign policy can be very easily regarded by citizens in terms of national interest, because these things are fundamentally unlike the private concerns most familiar and preoccupying to citizens. The "good" may be more readily identified in national terms than in local terms for this reason and for an additional but related one: the evaluation is inevitably in somewhat more abstract terms. In the national scene the citizen may somewhat assume the philosopher's task of describing the good in general terms, while locally he more resembles the administrator in having to find the better cause to espouse in matters more particular. Also, the affairs of local government more often seem to resemble private affairs, although this resemblance is more assumed than real or made to appear real more frequently than serves the public interest.

That public morality is in general of a higher order than private morality is probably attributable in part to the fact that citizens are somewhat freer to be moral with respect to public matters. To enlist in wartime is a sort of ultimate act of devotion which one can perform only in behalf of government, and of course one may die for his country only once. In private life the problem is rather the maintenance of the highest standard that may be constantly held. There one's personal interests press hard, with competitors having much to do with feasible standards. In matters not so directly impinging and in fields not so circumscribed one may defer more to the ideal.

Citizens who are not officials or workaday politicians are naturally most preoccupied with private concerns. When they attend briefly to public matters, they are prone to consider them in private-interest terms. This is particularly true in the public matters closest to them, where local familiarity invites reliance on the familiar private interest. Reputable citizens who are especially influential because of private eminence thus account for more frustration of the public interest, in local government particularly, than they themselves even begin to suspect.

There is no greater fallacy, and none more hostile to public morality, than the notion especially common to local affairs, although not confined to them, that "government is just a big business." The conception of "business-type corporations in government" flouts the fact that the peculiar virtue of such organizations must inhere in their governmental character.

Despite the deference democratic government properly gives private associations and their interests, the unique and crucial elements of public interest are to be differentiated from them. Variations in the quality of governmental performance according to levels, jurisdictions, and agencies turn principally upon the success with which this differentiation is made. Governmental actions which merely reflect or mildly translate private moralities are the sources of most dissatisfaction and frustration of private citizens in their public upreaching. Only politicians, political officials, and public-administrative personnel have consistent responsibilities for pursuit of primarily public ends. Great numbers of persons in public-administrative posts, either because of immersion in specialized tasks and environmental elements overwhelmingly private or because of easy movement back and forth between public and private assignments, have only rudimentary awareness of their peculiarly public responsibilities. Under pressures most constantly private and in the difficulties of reconciling private and public concerns, values distinctly public are greatly obscured.

The morality of democratic government in its administrative aspects turns first of all, then, on orientation to the uniquely public interest. It turns on responsibility, controllability, and process related to that interest, leaving other value questions to determination in the political processes. Therefore, subsequent chapters of this discussion treat the following subjects: ordinary venality as only partially differentiated from private wrongdoing, law as one specialized aspect of the problem of process, administrative responsibility to courts and legislatures, responsibility epitomized in the chief executive, limitations on the values of administration as organizational performance, the problem of pressure groups as peculiarly posing the public-private conflict, the loyalty problems involving conflicts in standards individually held by officials and standards of the public organization, and the pattern of responsibility generally emerging from the entire discussion.

III

VENALITY IN GOVERNMENT

IN early societies the beginnings of culture and the beginnings of governance alike involved the establishment of special privilege for a few. Under harsh and primitive conditions, none could move much toward cultivation of the higher human potentialities except a few who by some kind of levy on the many were given leisure or special functional responsibilities which freed them from much of the direct burden of attaining mere subsistence. Special provision for the few was at that stage highly progressive, even though the privilege conferred was not invariably or responsibly used for society's advancement. Princely houses in the Orient continue out of that primitive system, and many other less dramatic survivals permeate the patterns of privilege and responsibility.

At even later stages the price of governance was one that today would also appear as graft and corruption. Dr. Sun Yat-sen in China, with high moral purpose directed to the unification and democratization of China, could derive funds for a central government only through provincial governors. Much money and nondemocratic privilege adhered to these tax collectors, and this feature was an open, recognized part of the system. Lingering effects of entrenched privilege also are reflected in a tendency in the Chinese legal system to reveal and to decide according to the might of litigants. In some Latin-American states today it is popularly assumed as a matter of course that the taxgatherer will become wealthy. In authoritarian states it is taken for granted that all in power will gain disproportionate and unaudited perquisites.

All feudal systems involved grants or protections of privilege in hierarchies of privilege, a frank, rough-and-ready reliance on special influence and power, governance being achieved as a function of an association of power groupings thus established and supported. Vestiges of the system linger on in class entitlements to membership in legislative houses and to administrative posts. The latter entitlement gradually has come to be associated with, and to an extent legitimatized by, higher educational attainments; but this also has continued to reflect more or less association with class status, its virtue in part the virtue of *noblesse oblige*. D. B. Eaton, in describing the reform movement ushering in the British Civil Service system, used language suggesting that in the earlier market place where governance had to be bought by the public, some such favoritisms were the price required by especially effective, restricted publics.

Fiction and the literature of scholarship alike present pictures of profligate privilege in kingly and papal courts, diminishing generally and gradually after the Renaissance but still highly extravagant in any modern view so late as the government of Napoleon, some of his contemporaries, and their royal successors. It would appear that it has been in the rise of democracy—itself a phenomenon based on moral thought associated with mass self-interest—that we may see clarification and elevation of the public's moral expectations and the morality of governmental practice.

The National Government

Starting when it did, and starting as a democracy, government in the United States began at a relatively high moral level. Our problems of morality have appeared here from the beginning in democratic and rather modern contexts. They have had to do quite particularly with the moralities of popular government and in their advancing pattern are extremely subtle. Perhaps this subtlety inheres in part in the fact that they must be viewed currently and in terms of greater total governmental scope. But certainly it arises also in a substantial translation from involvement with gross privilege, exploitation, and venality to involvement with the more general and complicated consideration of popular responsiveness and responsibility.

Of course we have had our dramatic excesses in flagrant cases of outright venality, but they have been relatively small in content and relatively infrequent. These in forms old and new we shall have throughout the unfolding future, always serving to refine further our expectations, institutions, and practices. But from the beginning the moral bounds have been here more restricted than those of other periods under other governmental systems.

At the national level, in backward look, it seems amazing that a government thus emergent from an older history has kept, so generally, well within the bounds set by the most familiar criteria of morality. Much is owed of course to Washington and the standards he set. Much is owed to the great colleagues of the formative period. We have had no President of proved depravity, none, in spite of Grant and Harding, whom we do not feel to have been distinguished on the whole by a great deal of honorable devotion. The record would indicate that even in Harding's case the responsibility of the presidency quickly heightened the responsibility of the man. On the federal bench, in Congress, and in the executive branch generally, notwithstanding some lamentable exceptions, the level of performance has been so high as to give us basic confidence in our in-

stitutions and as to provide a story of great human advance.
This record is not an exclusive one; it is a part of the general record of democratic government. But it is well for
Americans to recall it, lest their need for constant watchful-
ness and the bitterness and heat often exhibited in partisan
conflict should appear to suggest much less virtue than we
have.

This general record is a product of politics, as an out-
growth of popular government. And of course many of
the failures have been political concessions rather than examples of personal venality on the part of responsible officials
such as Grant and Harding. This double meaning of "politics" contributes greatly to the confusion of popular discussions in which democracy is revered, politics and politicians reviled.

Lincoln as postmaster in Illinois granted petty special
favors which minutely defrauded the government. But
Lincoln lives forever as one of the great moral leaders in
history. His conduct of his post office reflected the embry-
onic public-service viewpoint of his time; in the general
run his handling of even that office was rather superior. He
would not have sold his vote in Congress as Webster substantially did, and Webster's performance, in part on a very
high plane, was well within the outer limits of the public
moral standards of his day. The Websters in our history were
never numerous enough or unprincipled enough really to
invalidate the body of Congress as a responsible vehicle of
the effective moral sentiments of the time. As a legislature,
Congress has served generally according to the limited
Rousseau formula of approaching the "general will," afford-
ing a means to cancel out many of the pluses and minuses of
the "will of all." This is not enough, of course. But the
shortcoming is a lack of truly public-interest statesman-
ship, not a substantial yielding to common venality.

Some congressmen, it is true, yield to the lure of head-lines waiting the obstreperous who figure not in the un-dramatic business of reconciliation by which majority gov-ernment is achieved. And a considerable number will con-fess privately on occasion that they vote against their own evaluation of the merits of a particular measure in order to assert the "independence of Congress" or "to force the President to pay more attention to us." Just so do less com-petent executives sometimes insist upon modification of sound and satisfactory proposals of subordinates in order "to show who's boss." These practices injure the prestige of Congress and lower the level of its performance. There is also a much too exclusive preoccupation with parochial concerns of individual constituencies, resulting in too much bloc government and too little or too unsuccessful public-interest policy.

But the parochial concern is at least a concern with an immediate public, and failure beyond that is not so much a failure of Congress as a reflection of an absence of comple-mentary, supporting political machinery. All these matters relate to rather nice subleties of political morality. While it has had venal members, at the level of sheer venality Con-gress as a body has never approached the brink. Generally it has been reluctant to provide its own fair rewards for the heavy burdens it bears. This reluctance traces directly to concern about popular attitudes, and even if this is seen as merely fear of popular retribution, it testifies to the effec-tiveness of popular expectations.

In the executive bureaucracy, the same forces have pro-duced a systematized handling of rewards which in higher levels is generally felt to fall seriously below the responsi-bilities of the posts. As for ordinary venality which could corrupt such a system, remembering the fierce scrutiny of the opposition party, Congress in general, the press, and watchful interest groups, and mindful of how little has been revealed or even charged in proportion to the dimensions of the business handled, one must conclude that the record represents for large undertakings an all-time high in history.

The bureaucracy is most susceptible to such corruption as is being discussed, during war. Emergency operations of the greatest urgency and swiftest increase in dimensions tax every capacity, including the moral. To government employment come hordes of citizens not schooled in the special responsibilities of public service, not understanding the moral protections of bureaucratic work ways, not able to anticipate the pitfalls, and tending to regard private interest as too closely approximating the public interest. They come carrying a readiness to grant favors, to cut friends in on a good thing, which taken for granted as part of the way of free enterprise, is reckoned as corrupt in government business. The performance of the special war bureaucracy in World War II was not typical of "the government" and marked the low points of public performance in the last twenty-five years.

Yet the general moral level of the war performance was by far the highest in our war history. The great war loss was in waste attributable to urgency, in which others would have done no better than those who had responsibility. Actual corruption undoubtedly was only a fractional percentage of the business done. Indeed, a noted consultant to industry, serving the government during the war as an expert in administration, complained that the government was wasteful in the lengths to which it went to prevent and eliminate venality. "In business we spend no more when we get that kind of thing down to a small decimal percentage; it costs more than it is worth to go further," he said. "In government you don't stop at that decimal; you don't care how much you spend to get it to fantastically low decimals." The effort, out of political concern as well as official morality, is not merely to avoid graft but to conserve the moral capital of the nation.

Before complicating the picture by considering state and local government in similar terms, it may be well to attempt a preliminary appraisal of some of the reasons which go to explain the extraordinarily high moral level maintained in the national government.

Mention already has been made of the public scrutiny turned on the national government. It is a scrutiny beyond imagining for those in private business. It is a scrutiny that subjects officials to ready blackmail, even when they are innocent of wrongdoing. Single individuals may start vendettas which may easily ruin all but the strongest and most eminent. Strong suspicion of wrongdoing carries grievous penalities for the individual directly concerned, penalties for all his superiors, and indeed for the administration at large. Even those inured to state politics are startled to find when they come into the national arena how hot and unrelenting is the public searchlight there.

Thus, the first deterrent is in politics, the fear of public disfavor. The second may be in the political dimensions of national business. A favor granted in one special quarter can buy very little in the general political scene, may indeed invite political opposition from all those who would feel equally entitled to it, and there are many more of them in the nation than there are in a smaller jurisdiction. In other words, a special favor, the inducement to which would be political gain, produces so many political liabilities that these tend to outweigh both its political and personal attractions. In this area, size is a factor working for the public interest.

A third deterrent is in system. Older citizens recall the free-and-easy days when railway conductors on some of the better runs appeared to attain to rather remarkable affluence. Nowadays fares and tickets are collected by pairs of trainmen as checks upon each other, and they use forms designed to make auditing enforce responsibility. There are spotters, too, and the fear of observant patrons as tipsters. In the restaurant or cafeteria one employee issues the patron his dinner check, while another collects from him, the two transactions being carried on with paper forms which lend themselves to checking both operations and the two against each other. In the national government such techniques are much further developed than anywhere else: the technique of group judgment, of organizational handling, a sharing of access to transactions; the technique of full records; the technique of dividing, not among individuals merely, but among units and large, separately responsible organizations the actions of certifying, paying, reviewing, auditing, and investigating. Somewhere in such a chain someone will see the sign of irregularity. The chain is characteristic not merely of money transactions, where it would not be so unusual or so significant, since the great majority of federal personnel in the course of long careers see no public money except their personal pay checks. The chain—and it is a much more complicated arrangement than a chain—is characteristic of the handling of all national governmental business. Organizational method consequently provides normally the value of the board form and other values of process unsuspected by those not intimately acquainted with it. These are values associated with the functioning of public hierarchies. Alongside this system tipsters and gossips and the suspicious abound, and many tens of millions of dollars are spent annually on investigations occasioned by mere whispers of irregularity.

The factors of system are partly a product of the

scientific-management movement, partly a result of the more general movement for better administration, but chiefly a product of political concern.

The virtue that these factors together indicate is, then, primarily institutional and societal, not simple reflections of personal rectitude. It turns on the presence of sufficient political officers to enforce political responsibility. Jackson's espousal of the spoils system had at least the morality of crudely emphasizing political responsiveness and responsibility. It was moral also in seeking public recruitment as against class recruitment or the vested-interest aspect of tenure.

There is a professional responsibility, too—although this is by no means wholly salutary—of economists to the economic discipline, of lawyers to legal standards, and so on. And there is rectitude as well. No one knows how much of this there is when institutions and techniques provide so many bulwarks to personal integrity. But the informed know of the high, self-sacrificing devotion of many in key posts; and the better informed know of the zealous, conscientious loyalty found in the great bulk of the rank and file. There is in this a special kind of integrity, a special devotion to government as a profession, and a devotion to the government as the government. It is a special and constant kind of patriotism. There is a great deal of self-selection in the development of government personnel that the system does not wholly account for; great numbers of people seek government employment out of a search for an especially worthy object of their service.

Not even the muckrakers, famous at the turn of the century, could seriously and directly impugn the national government. In spite of revelations of many reprehensible actions by national officials in recent years, we may believe that these are highly unusual. Crude wrongdoing is not a major, general problem of our government. Further moral advance turns upon more complicated and elevated concerns.

That the absence of venality in these terms is no index of the morality that is crucial is suggested by the record of Germany. Allowing for the fact that the German government in the period just before Hitler reflected many social attitudes not conforming to our own standards, it is a fair statement that through those years the German governmental practice was in high degree free from what is generally thought of as corruption. Yet just a few years later that very government lent itself readily to as thorough a renunciation of values as modern history has seen. The morality with which we must be most concerned is of an order far higher.

State and Local Government

The muckrakers did, however, reveal a shoddy picture in some of our states and cities of a half-century ago. The present state of government at these levels is publicly revealed only by an unorganized procession of news stories reflecting much less interest and scrutiny than are directed to the national government. It is difficult to generalize about the forty-eight states or the thousands of local governmental jurisdictions. Malheur County, Oregon, with its vast area and its handful of people, is hardly comparable in any way with Cook County, Illinois. Constitutions, charters, structure, institutions, laws, and practice vary so greatly that in contrast the complex national government is a simple thing. It does seem clear that while area differences in practice would have some relationship to area values, such differences in governmental practice would give no fair index to the moral differences among the areas. In some respects, great size of the jurisdiction affects performance *unfavorably*. In large cities opportunities to profit from un-ethical performance are greatest. Yet metropolitan govern-ment today is generally much better than it was in 1900.

Some three decades ago a Tammany politician, George Washington Plunkitt, made a series of speeches, including one called "Honest Graft and Dishonest Graft," in which he defended, without much effective evidence of political vulnerability, such practices as those involving personal profit for officials in buying on inside information property soon to be desired for public use. No case of the sort has been brought to light in New York for years, and now no New York politician would dare to defend such a practice. Not long ago, cases of exactly the same kind were aired in Chi-cago, with no sign of political penalty resulting; yet Chicago, too, has been making progress.

A real two-party system, with the outcome of every elec-tion in a particular jurisdiction in doubt, suggests itself as a factor maximizing the effects of good politics and minimiz-ing the effects of bad politics. There is no such system in a number of states and in many local jurisdictions. Certainly the morality of New York City government has improved, not merely as Tammany's hold on the Democratic party has weakened, but more as election outcomes have become rather consistently uncertain. Doubtful jurisdictions more readily discipline corruption.

Size of population in a jurisdiction in some respects seems to be one factor *favoring* morality. In a small jurisdiction common acquaintance with what is done is too readily felt to be an adequate check on officials who often come from, or come to be, an entrenched and privileged special pub-lic. In a large jurisdiction, given appropriate structures and political processes, the canceling out of contradictory special interests and the minimization of the importance of many special interests appear to contribute, in certain respects at least, to better performance. Where very large special interests develop in large jurisdictions, in racial and religious groupings or in industrial groupings, the outcome is more complicated and less clear, sometimes appearing to be a minority dominance, sometimes a sort of political and insufficiently representative majority dominance. In general, cosmopolitanism seems to be an important characteristic making for governmental virtue. Multiplication of governmental activities, causing a kind of cosmopolitanism in government itself, also seems to put officials in stronger moral positions, enabling them to withstand temptation and pressure on a number of fronts in the strength of their popular service on many fronts.

But local government comes close to its constituents, and it is in the nature of politics to try to please. This leads to a tendency to bend the general practice to the particular person. There is a general tendency for the popularly elected assessor to value all property at less than its legal value. If he should yield equally to this tendency in all cases, no inequity would result within his jurisdiction, although revenues locally collected for other jurisdictions would be inequitably raised as among jurisdictions. The tendency, however, is for the elected assessor also to shade valuations somewhat according to the influence of the property owner. In general, homes of the poor are assessed at much more nearly their true worth than are homes of the more well to do.

This kind of corruption tends somewhat to characterize local government, but perhaps it is less than wholly corrupt; insofar as it reflects ability of government nicely to adjust to individuals, the practice may cover some actions positively virtuous, but in this direction virtue turns readily to vice.

It is an interesting fact, if fact it is, that the very intimacy between citizen and local government invites some corruption of government. Certain it is that there is more mediocre government in America in the counties than anywhere else and more in the municipalities than in the other levels of government. Even where there is relatively little corruption there is much administrative slovenliness. It may be that not merely intimacy is involved so much as function, however. Municipal government has to deal directly with the social conditions and phenomena in which racketeers find their opportunities. Citizens outside the law tend to corrupt the law and its agencies. Those dealing with the national government are more often the legitimate enterprises which at worst strain at the boundaries of the legitimate rather than acting in outright opposition to it. Big businesses were the most meticulous observers of war controls; perhaps they had too much at stake to court the disaster of clear violation of law. When they encounter trouble with the national government it is usually on a question open to technical differences in interpretation or in connection with policy definition previously accepted as valid but no longer necessarily so.

At all events, there do appear to be certain factors making for a higher kind of morality in certain aspects of bigness, private and public. The larger public approaches more nearly the public interest than does the smaller public. An agricultural-relief act extending benefits to millions of farmers is more virtuous than a special benefit bestowed upon one farmer, not merely because the law has resulted from the processes requisite to enactment, but because the general benefit has lost much special-benefit character; it will have been conceived and publicly defended in terms of social equity. Responsibility to a larger public tends to make for performance in larger-public terms.

Perhaps in part because dominance is easier and more simply to be achieved in smaller jurisdictions, there are still many areas of local government in which a small group of privately eminent citizens, as private citizens, largely dominate government and inject into it chiefly private standards simply because they are familiar to the group. A few lawyers in association with a few businessmen often constitute the effective but rather anonymous political machine, and in such jurisdictions the public morality is little more elevated than the private.

There are municipalities, however, where political and governmental structure has been much improved, opening the way to readier response to minority complaint and to readier determination of majority position and thereby diminishing the effect of private interests and developing distinctly civic character. Those cities where city managers are strong are generally excellent examples, although the presence of the managers and their ability to serve well is probably more an effect of civic health than its cause. Great advances have been made since the days of Steffens, even though there are other great strides to be taken to bring local government up to the public expectations of today. Many reforms will be required, many of them subtle. In the meantime the voting record which shows greatest citizen interest in national elections challenges the common sentiment that local government is spontaneously and inevitably better than the other levels of government because it is so readily and naturally the people's own.

Among the states there are wide differences in the qualities of functional performances and in the tools and resources available to their officials. New York, where responsibility of the governor long has been established generally in the pattern recommended by the Hoover Commission for the presidency, is probably the most uniformly advanced state government. Among the important factors would appear to be constitutional structure, long practice, the achievements of a succession of unusually able governors attracted by the facilities of the office and its opportunities, a very large and very cosmopolitan population, and highly developed political instruments open to the public in a consistently two-party field where elections swing readily from side to side.

Other than New York few states have developed organization and administration or political institutions generally as effective as those of the national government. For a good many, thoroughgoing constitutional, political, and administrative changes are long overdue. But while there are some bad spots, they offer no picture like that Steffens and his colleagues disclosed a half-century ago. What the muckrakers found tied back to bad city conditions, and some of the worst state situations today tie to relatively bad, if generally improved, city situations. Others are related more to rotten-borough practices, franchise perversions, long ballots, restricted participation in party functions, and other such arrangements.

Throughout the nation in state and local government tens of thousands of citizens express civic devotion with hope of no particular reward except prestige or a sense of influence and participation. Even in Chicago many among the ward aldermen and district leaders are net losers in their expenditure of money, time, and energy.

At state- and local-government levels, too, in some areas, we appear to be beyond the corruption long associated with government in the minds of many citizens. In all areas the advance is fairly persistent in that kind of quality. This advance has taken place in a half-century in which public employees of state and local government have increased in number more than those of the national government, if we exclude war and war-related activities of the national government. In other words, we have bigger government and yet more moral government than we used to have. We have bigger government, and better government in this respect, and yet it is said that our society, because of the irresponsibility associated with mobility, urbanization, weakening of the family, and weakening of the hold of churches, has been deteriorating morally.

Factors of Progress

We cannot be at all confident that private morality has deteriorated until studies such as those attempted two decades ago in *Recent Social Trends* are expanded and continued in comparative terms. It may be doubted that the common pessimism is warranted. It may be that government extends a private moral advance. But in the face of uncertainty on this score, we might speculate concerning other factors contributing to the clear improvement of elemental morality in governmental performance. At least two additional and related ones are worth mentioning here.

A corrupt Boston boss of the muckraker days defended himself and his practice to Steffens by citing the service his organization extended citizens. It was a crude but direct social service, providing a political social life, helping the unemployed to jobs, providing relief, giving aid in misfortune and illness. This function was characteristic of other machines besides the one in Boston. It was no less systematic than incidence of the burden and distribution of the benefits of private benevolence by individuals, church, lodge, and neighborhoods according to the pattern then common. But the city machine's program was financed by graft, at public expense. The defense of the Boston boss was that "the people don't want justice, they want help."

The suggestion in this is that the improvement in governmental morality may be in some way and in some degree a direct reflection of a shift in governmental functions. Government has increasingly combined the dispensations of justice *and* help. The levy upon the public for social service has been systematized and legalized, and the distribution of the service has been legitimatized, made a public reponsibility instead of a direct party activity, organized in the direction of equity, and improved in quality and effectiveness. Coincidentally the corrupt machine has been deprived of much of the popular support of its corruption.

A second and more generalized factor reflecting the first has been a general building up of the political that is good. Officials, parties, and governmental organizations have learned, under the pounding of reformers, press, schools, churches, and public. This learning is substantially beyond the consciousness of individual officials and politicians but has been translated gradually into structures and practices as an improved inheritance for successive incumbents. Some of what was earlier surplusage of political idealism has been incorporated into our moral political capital.

Since this is also the course by which we may advance further, it is desirable to dwell upon the distinction between the political in a good sense and the political in a bad sense.

In its good sense the political is related to the process of identifying and establishing positions acceptable to, and advantageous for, the public. Once democracy is selected as the basic political scheme, we must accept political processes as the vehicle by which whatever morality the public requires may be revealed and achieved. Our concern is with relatively better political processes. The moral failings of which the public is aware occur in concessions to the political through relatively worse political processes.

We see confusion of the two meanings in newspaper attacks upon political leaders when these leaders are charged with presenting programs "simply to win votes." Such attacks heap contempt upon politicians and politics. Yet the attempt of leaders to win votes for a program is essential to the moral values associated with democracy. Attacks upon that attempt as such are attacks upon democracy. The role of democratic leadership is at once to defer to popular desires and to try to lead those desires; in either aspect of the role it is a search for popular support, and this search is basically political good. In the refinement of moral considerations we may ask: "Win what votes reflecting what moral values?" "Win votes in what way?" This is the search for identification and ostracism of the political bad. We must continually press for the distinction, lest when we throw out the bath water we throw out the baby, too. To follow as a simple recipe of governmental reform the counsel to "take it out of politics" is to set forth on the road to democratic suicide, and there are dangerous if unknowing inclinations in that direction. When any function or process is relatively taken out of politics, it should be done reflectively, cautiously, and taken out not so far that it may not readily be drawn in again for public correction.

When an individual official profits privately by some wrongdoing in his post, he provides an example of governmental corruption; but when his act is one as likely to occur in a nongovernmental post, it is hardly to be regarded as a political phenomenon. It rates as such at all only because of the premium we are disposed to put upon public morality—and the existence of this premium is significant. But his action is not especially or characteristically related to the way of politics.

The line at which the political bad begins clearly to appear is where the characteristic political effort to win votes is exerted in an evil way. Systematized graft is more politically significant than individual frailty because it involves a general corruption of government. More, it usually is related to efforts to get the political support of the small, special public implicated in the graft. Because it is also a granting of special favors to a few at the cost of the many, it is political bad multiplied. When the favors go to an illegitimate public, such as one engaged in illegal gambling, it becomes political bad raised to the nth degree.

On the other hand, a special favor, in administration even —as by a traffic policeman, to a blind person or a cripple— would be regarded as political good when it appears an act of equity compensating for underprivilege. When the benefit is a legislated grant it is doubly political good because the legislative enactment reflects systematic consideration of the equities involved.

Any disposal of governmental benefits which if known would be regarded as disproportionate and undue is political bad. What is "disproportionate" is crucially subject to changing interpretation, and this interpretation is the area of official and citizen difficulty. Paraphrasing E. A. Ross, concern develops in the gap between the new social situation and emerging public expectations, on the one hand, and a controlling morality and institutional arrangements making this morality controlling, on the other hand. The historically familiar immorality of governmental venality is at least as well controlled as equivalent, familiar immoralities of private associations. Emerging and outreaching concerns have to do with moral refinements. These in democracy are distinguished by their reference to equity conceived in more and more public, mass-interest terms in opposition to special privilege. They are similarly distinguished by their reference to individualization and pluralism. Reconciling and applying these somewhat contradictory and yet related values in a changing world in the light of developing insights is the continuing business of politics, including public administration. This is the effort to convert the political good into the political better by elimination of the newly recognized political bad.

Concern for equity in unqualified mass-interest terms would drive us toward absolute equalitarianism, in which mass interest would not be dynamically served. If complete economic equality were feasible, differences in status, power, and influence would remain incident to organization and might be expected to be more concentrated and aggravated than under a certain economic differentiation. Even the ideal of political equality does not require uniform possession of influence or power among citizens. Absolute equality in both economic and political power, if conceivable at all, must be considered as requiring as its price a vast surrender of pluralism and social dynamism. We are not here concerned with a morality which would diminish dynamics, but rather with one which would maximize their values in truly public terms. There would appear to be little basis for the belief that either *laissez faire* or equalitarianism along lines illustrated in New Zealand has any such maximizing potential. Systematic study of incentives to disclose what differences in income actually generate dynamism would appear to provide an important frontier now open to scholars, and more systematic application of incentives affords a frontier opening to politics and political management.

At all events, it is to be recognized that no matter how far we may go in advancing concern for the equitable public interest at large, differences in influence will remain as implicit in democratic pluralism as in social and political organization. The significant thing is that these differences will be weighed and controlled by democratic means.

Differences in influence inevitably will require "purchases" of crucial support as a price of that kind of order. Such purchases are, and will continue to be, the concessions necessary to agreements possible only through compromise achieved by the not wholly equal. Such concessions are familiar and largely accepted without much thought or criticism in all private associations. Similar concessions, especially visible and dramatic in political order, are sometimes considered by the naïve as peculiar to government. This attitude is revealed by contemptuous attacks upon "power politics," "efforts to win votes," and anything at all identified as a "political deal." A consequence of pluralism is that special influences figure in equations leading to decisions. On our pluralistic planet it is inconceivable that for many decades the populations of India and China can exercise world influence proportionate to the size of their populations. In the refinement of world politics, however, their influence will rise. Within nations, in varying ways and degrees, differences in influence as between groups and individuals will be associated with differentiations in status, functions, interests, location, and traits. These differences in influence will be modified and minimized at the dictates of new standards, insights, and feasibilities.

Democratic morality seeks, not the complete elimination of special influence, but its refinement in terms of democratic values. This implies whatever reductions in special privilege as seem to be relevant, necessary, and feasible, and the opening of opportunity for the largest realization of the potentialities of citizens generally. It implies the progressive elimination of those prices paid for special influence which in new insight appear venal, wasteful, or discriminatory. It implies making the exercise of power both more responsive and more responsible in whatever respects and degrees seem appropriate and effective in changing time and circumstance. In particular this points to clarifying responsibility of government to the general public and to developing the popular character of the politically effective.

Moral performance begins in individual self-discipline on

the part of officials, involving all that is meant by the word "character." But this is not enough. It also requires systematic process which supports individual group judgment enriched by contributions from persons variously equipped and concerned, and differentiations in responsibilities particularly designed to relate these responsibilities to each other and to a whole-public responsibility. The official individually and organizationally must be concerned to go beyond simple honesty to a devoted guardianship of the continuing reality of democracy.

Beyond these requirements are still others—those of citizenship. Self-discipline of citizens with respect to government is too little stressed. For citizens, too, there must be systematic arrangements supporting character in their performance. Also, citizens need to defer more readily to the contributions of citizens differently equipped and situated. They need to strive more often and more consciously to relate their personal concerns to public concerns and to help perfect arrangements supporting these citizen responsibilities.

These ends may be advanced through changing popular and official expectations, through new political institutional arrangements, through new and improved administrative arrangements. At crucial moments and in crucial aspects they will be formulated and organically incorporated in government by enactments of law. Concentrated attention given to law as a subject has converted it for some into a symbol of the whole of due process in administration. In the next chapter this legalistic approach to administration will be examined.

IV

AN ADMINISTRATIVE VIEW
OF LAW

CONTROL of public administration is pinned at one point to the chief executive, at another to the legislature, and at another to the courts. Since the present discussion concentrates on executive responsibility, including that of the chief executive, executive relationship to the other two branches of government can be only generally treated. In a shorthand approach, law, as the product of the legislature, as the peculiar material of that form of administration which is especially based in the courts, as the basis for other, general administration, and as a specialized symbol of good process, may be used as a tie of relationship.

The very public which may view Congress most critically, even contemptuously, tends to have an abstract reverence for its product—law. That reverence is both heightened and particularized as it extends to the juridic process and to the courts, to which seem to be attributed a quite exclusive responsibility and capacity for lawful governmental action. The revered phrase "due process" has only legalistic implications, by no means commensurate with the totality of democratic governmental action. When extension of the values symbolized by the phrase is proposed, extension is conceived in legalistic terms. Yet since long before the Founding Fathers, no statesmen have considered even momentarily restricting governmental actions generally to those taken through, or subject to, juridic process. Law in its revered sense, the courts, and their process are obviously not sufficient repositories of our concern for morality in public administration.

Many citizens, however, tend to feel that if only the government took all its actions in the due process of the courts, the political millennium would have come. They thus seek to pour all law and all good process into one mold. They ignore so simple a fact as the volume of law and the volume of legalistic process it would require if there were only one appropriate process. They take no account of the fact that much of the volume of law is what they readily perceive in the private world to be simple decision making in the course of doing business. They exclaim over the number of "Executive Orders," failing to see that there is rarely significant difference between these and presidential decisions conveyed by letter or telephone to an executive agency. This conduct of business in formal law and in administrative decision is bound to unfold, even with no recognizable changes in policy. There are other important misconceptions of more complicated content, arising out of the failure to regard the government as necessarily pluralistic in process in variously serving plural interests.

A great deal of confusion has been caused by some tendency to use "rule making" as somehow generally synonymous with public administration or even as naming and describing a principal sector of public administration. The tendency developed among persons trained in law, and the term inevitably is interpreted as involving a process more hard and fast, more fundamentally coercive even though related to concern for due process, and more legalistic than practice is or should be. As a process of producing or acting according to precise, formal and specific guides for conduct, rule making does not constitute more than 2 or 3 per cent of the total area comprehended by public administration. By far the greater part of the field is occupied by the exercise of discretion within the general bounds fixed by laws and regulations. If "rule making" is defined in the broadest possible terms as meaning carrying on affairs according to some plan or system, in a habitual or generally understood course or manner of procedure, one might as well refer to private administration or to the conduct of an orchestra or of a household as "rule making." So used, the term has no real meaning, but the effect of its use is to support practices which encourage rigidity, the force of habit, and the weakness of imagination which are three handmaidens of mediocrity, as they are also of system.

The need for standards is real. The need for systematic handling of public business is real. But useful standards can be only general guides, and the best systems will exist in general arrangements, will have much informal character and flexibility, and will tax discretion all the way. To talk of the reality as rule making twists and demeans thought about public administration as it would to discuss the performance of an orator in terms of grammar and rhetoric.

The present discussion makes no pretension to specialist competence in the field of law, and there is no intention here to treat in any balanced or comprehensive way the functions of courts, jurists, and attorneys in the juridic area. Just as lawyers and courts have discussed general public administration, the proposal here is to deal with law and the procedural notions of lawyers from the special point of view of public administration. Insofar as the juridic process and point of view are considered critically, it is not the purpose to challenge them in their own house but in another. It is intended to suggest their limitations and inapplicability in other governmental areas. It is meant to insist that the other areas of action are very much larger than the areas of the juridic, and their necessities much more differentiated than legal literature has recognized.

Much of what is said or implied in criticism of the legal profession or its point of view could be said similarly with reference to other professions, but not with similar bearing on public administration. Perhaps everything that is said is familiar to some leaders in fields of legal scholarship and theory. Certainly what is said would create no great stir within a few law faculties. But little effort has been made in print to look critically at the common pretensions of law to comprehensive and almost final significance in public administration.

Juridic and Executive Law

The early development of courts and their long association with the development of popular legislatures provide convincing testimony to the existence of problems involved in the application of law far beyond the ubiquitous problem of communication through language. If such limited clarification of its own intent as would be possible in further language was all that had been involved, the legislature might have been felt to be fully capable of making its own clarifications. This in fact it often does in successive modifications. But the intent of law, both before and after such modifications, is to provide a basis for administration. Administration is ever a means to policy making beyond the capacity of legislatures to achieve in their enactments.

In one aspect this intent is to provide a basis for adjudication, which is one facet of administration. In another and larger aspect the intent is to provide a basis for executive administration. In this second aspect there is sometimes in an uncertain and varying degree expectation of some subsequent adjudication of some aspects of executive administration. In most governments the courts have never assumed or been assigned a position at all approaching complete or uniform right of juridic review of all executive action. In democratic as in other systems the great body of executive action is not effectively reviewable by courts and not intended to be so reviewable.

In the beginnings of our present institutions courts constituted a part of the executive agency of the royal sovereign, expressing and enforcing his will. Insofar as his purpose included administration of justice in the sense we now attribute to the term, the courts administered justice. Even in such terms the unifying functional description of the courts would have been as agencies of law enforcement. But they did much more than administer justice. As agencies of law enforcement they conducted a substantial part of the executive business of government, imposing the sovereign will in diverse ways.

The ceremony and ritual bulwarking royal authority thus came to characterize all the various kinds of business handled by the courts. The style endures as a façade of the juridic structure as it later evolved, and it is even now sometimes too readily accepted as testifying to the juridic essence.

Many traces remain of the early pattern mingling executive and judicial functions. In some of our states county courts still exercise some of the chief-executive functions elsewhere transferred long ago to executive boards of supervisors. In some areas agencies of this kind retain the name but little of the modern character of courts. Another example is found in the nominal retention by grand juries of the function of inspecting poor farms and other administrative operations, a function now of slight and rare significance in that repository. The lingering notion that prosecutors and sheriffs are officers of the court gives these now independent figures an unwarranted haven under the court's halo, fogging over some of the poorest of official performances and confusing responsibility. For another example of the carry-over, it may be recalled that so recently as in colonial America the courts were inducting citizens into local militias. The courts generally, even now, carry on primarily administrative, rather than judicial, business in the fields of bankruptcies, reorganizations, and receiverships.

It has been commonly forgotten that the rise of popular legislatures and the general growth of democracy have been accompanied by a withdrawal from the courts of many executive responsibilities for enforcement of the sovereign will. The associated enrichment of the conceptual content of justice has led to greater and greater development and specialization of the strictly juridic procedure, and its clearer confinement to areas peculiarly appropriate to that procedure. Alongside these two developments was a third, reflecting, and opening the way to fuller reality of the fact that the sovereign will had become the popular will. This third development was the enlargement, variation, and enrichment of the processes of politics. The new sovereign was seeking new values through the juridic even while it insulated the juridic from many of the direct shocks of political contact. For the new sovereign similarly to have insulated the executive would have been to abdicate. The insulation of the courts from politics was therefore associated with confinement of the courts to narrower limits. Concurrently, the new sovereign was opening the executive area to politics, demanding that the new sovereign will be served through executive action appropriate to its unfolding purpose.

It is perhaps not surprising, but worth remark, that the change in sovereignties has been more thoroughly incorporated into public attitudes and understandings in Britain than in the United States. In our country the fear of government that gave rise to modern, democratic institutions has been largely carried over to fear of popular government, and the fear has been unconsciously but actively cultivated by scholars and citizens with legalistic preoccupations. Here a high percentage of the grist of juridic mills is brought to them on horses spurred by this fear, involving countless cases that would never reach British courts.

A step toward a less fearful but more truly critical attitude may be taken by further identifying two aspects of the intent of legislation as providing in the one aspect law governing court action and in the other a basis for executive administration. The two aspects are distinguishable, even if not—and not needing to be—everywhere clearly differentiated.

In some respects the distinction is to be found in the degree of immediacy and exclusiveness of reliance upon court decisions. But large areas of executive administration have never been at all, or seriously proposed to be, subject to judicial review. These areas seem to be related to a spasmodic and never fully expressed avoidance by the courts of direct challenge to the sovereign powers of the legislature which find necessary extension in executive action. Here, among democratic states, the basic responsibility and the basic safeguard have been felt to rest in the legislature. Popular legislatures have reserved the right to review and control nearly all policy made in the course of administration, whether juridic or executive. When, in states whose constitutions are single, written instruments, the courts have made policy contrary to legislative policy, the overriding power of the legislature is sometimes exercised by dint of ingenious invention and sometimes through the laborious and slow process of securing constitutional amendment.

It is the existence of the overriding power of the legislature which distinguishes democratic government. It may be said, somewhat extravagantly,* that the genius of the English common law—in contrast, for example, with Roman law—lies in the fact that it is based pragmatically on successive court decisions associated with a fluid and increasingly popular legislative control and not on a systematic, limiting, and overriding code. In the United States something of the same sort has been achieved through a flexibility in constitutional interpretation. Thus rising popular government has been enabled to substitute politics for royal prerogative as the basic control of law, and to grow on a basis of that substitution. According to A. B. White's classic little book *Self-Government at the King's Command*, royalty itself began to be party to the substitution as far back as the twelfth century.

At all events, nowhere more than in the British Commonwealth has the movement been to enthrone legislative control of law, nowhere less to enthrone juridic "law," and nowhere else has popular government demonstrated such flexibility and longevity. It is important and relevant in the United States, therefore, to consider law with reference to administration in these terms which subordinate both law and administration under law to politics.

In carrying forward our distinction between juridic law and executive law, it is useful to see how two branches of government serve to enlarge upon the product of the third branch in converting statutes into action.

The real meaning of a law appears only in the course of its administration. It is only as assessments are made, for example, that there is any demonstration of what revenue a tax law will provide and what burdens it will impose. Citizens who study and use the technical provisions of the income-tax law

* The common law did tend, under precedent, to assume the character of a code, and to enable the courts to become power centers highly resistant to legislative and popular control, and generating their own law. See Jerome Frank, *Law and the Modern Mind* (New York, 1934), 186–92.

aid the government in actually determining what the law is. After such determination the legislature may wish to modify the law in order to shift incidence. Thus arises talk of loopholes. The obligation of the executive branch is in many respects to participate and lead in this discovery of incidence; it also uses the technical provisions of the law in exercising its responsibility, and the law comes to be at the points fixed in the course of this competitive play of interest between citizen and government agency. In the course of this play of interest either competitor theoretically may seek adjudication in the courts on some points, and sometimes this is done in practice; but the practical area of no appeal from administrative decisions of the Bureau of Internal Revenue is very large, fully effective in tens of thousands of instances to one exception, and readily accepted by responsible tax attorneys. Wherever through action in any or all of these parts of the governmental continuum the incidence of law seems to have come to rest, the legislature identifies it, accepts it, or may be moved to new enactment.

Incidence of a law may and does change without legislation. Successive court decisions mark developments in interpretations of law growing out of administrative and citizen experience with its applications, and growing also out of changed meanings of language in changing social contexts. Here, too, the legislature may note these changes and may exercise or forgo its right of intervention.

The nonjudicial administrative branch also participates in this process of changing the incidence of existing law. It may see reason or opportunity for new application of the antitrust law, for example. Business concerns involved in one instance may be disposed to agree that their positions with respect to certain practices have weakened in the social scene and may consent to the new interpretation. In another instance the affected business concerns may appeal to the courts and lose. In either case there is a new determination of incidence, one achieved wholly by the executive branch, one by the executive and judicial together. In both cases the legislature either confirms by inaction or is moved to new enactment. It is part of the responsibilities of executive agencies and courts to keep the law up to date by searching experimentally for changing points of its effect.

A general purpose of law is to provide a reasonably stable basis for the orderly conduct of ordinary affairs. Always, the rule of law is also the rule of men responsible through institutions. Much of the administration of law is carried on privately. Many more determinations of action under law are made by individuals according to their own knowledge of law than are made by them on advice of counsel. Again, many more determinations are made on advice of counsel than by specific actions in the courts. These are made, subject to public determinations and in the light of public determinations already made. Affairs are conducted against a background of liability or opportunity for review and modification. This background provides a kind of process of successive appeal, limited in scope in one way in the case of the courts, limited in scope in another way in the executive agencies, and limited by cost in both branches. Because of the necessity for engaging attorneys for appeal to the courts and because of the formal and complicated character of that process, the cost of appeal for reconsideration administratively is generally much less. Because of this difference in cost and because administrative appeal is often much more effective and appropriate, it is far more frequently used by most citizens.

To develop the distinction between the scope of judicial appeal and administrative appeal, it may be useful to glance backward again to the days of very simple government. Outside of the collection of taxes and the conduct of war, administration of government had generally to do with the maintenance of means for the orderly conduct of business, such as implementing machinery for transferring title and enforcing contracts, and with breaches of the peace, very particularly with gross crime. The theories and processes of law were first and most systematically developed in these narrow terms.

Activities associated with the conduct of war and the levying and collection of taxes appeared from the beginning to be essential to the sovereign will and therefore peculiarly executive. Just so today does the Supreme Court consider war powers very cautiously and in the very broadest of the relatively new terms of constitutional law, usually postponing cases turning on war powers until the war is ended. In the field of real-estate and personal-property taxation, one of the oldest within government, the courts in some states have had little to do with the administrative function of assessment, although this is a function perhaps most widely, constantly, and for the longest time characterized by inequity and favoritism. The intrinsics of assessment are little affected by the law of officers, and in this field the courts continue to serve as in the beginning, principally to enforce collections.

The effect of inequity in property taxation tends to fall very heavily upon poor and uninfluential citizens, where inequity is compounded by relative incapacity to pay. Only when and where the stakes have become absolutely great in the income taxes of wealthy individuals and corporations have the lawyers generally and the courts as institutions entered the scene to insist upon due process and to clothe the process in juridic garb. In response to a very small, special public, only a few years ago the administrative Board of Tax Appeals was transformed into the Tax Court of the United States.

The point is that in early days of government the juridic

process developed especially to handle differences between citizens and to provide orderly arrangements for the conduct of private business. Not only property title and contracts of various kinds, but nuisances and crime were regarded as private business—the latter long being privately removed or avenged under the common law. For private differences, the government provided judicially gowned umpires and a procedure of complaint and defense.

The political content of the matters thus dealt with was relatively slight and relatively simple. Frank deference to the political nature of the business was generally limited to a restricted use of a popular jury—but only in the court of original jurisdiction, and there only in some types of cases —and to popular election of judges in some jurisdictions. Jury panels and jury "clubs" have sometimes been used by political organizations as a corruption of the juridic process, but generally the scope of juries has tended to be restricted to a diminishing proportion of the whole area, and growth in the movement toward bipartisan selection of judges and toward other insulating devices has tended to continue the court-process pattern outside the area of the more truly, and more highly charged, popular political.

"Due process" may be easily conceived and developed in these terms. But as the nuisance began to appear as more than an offense against a single neighbor and rather as an offense against the community, the umpiring process was not regarded as so often or so directly applicable; the community itself exercised a kind of right of eminent social domain to set up quarantines and sanitation standards. The test of process then turned largely to a test of the methods by which selectmen or councilmen were chosen and made accountable. Still later, as knowledge grew, the legislative bodies authorized health boards of expert character to protect the public interest under political control. Similarly, as

social standards were raised, zoning ordinances were enacted; and the possibility of appeal to the courts under such
ordinances quickly became not a matter of intrinsics but of
conformity with technical fact: Had notice of the zoning
been properly issued or had repairs to a substandard structure antedating zoning constituted enlargement and thus
subjected the owner to a charge of maintaining a nuisance?

A growing social sense that youths should not be tried and
punished in the familiar process by which adult offenders
were handled forced courts to give ground even in the
criminal field. For juvenile courts it still is difficult to find
judges sufficiently free from conventional legalistic thought
and ways, and the tendency is strong among those selected
to go back to umpiring the case presented by prosecutor and
defendant. Changing ideas about punishment by rule forced
the courts to retreat again, giving ground to parole boards
and experts in criminology. But the state-wide association of
judges in New Jersey not long ago conducted a heated campaign to support their demand for the return of the right to
fix sentences. They fought the cause of a vested interest in an
old process with an argument which was chiefly halo. In the
area of contention few other than partisans of the legalistic
fail to see executive handling as more truly due process.

The establishment of small-claims courts and special
courts for domestic relations cases represent two further re-
treats from the conventional juridic process in search of
something simpler, more flexible, and altogether more appropriate. Within traditional court patterns, too, concepts of
judicial review have undergone great modifications.

With the growth of knowledge, science, and public expectations, the principal development of government has
been in the strictly executive field. Where would the umpire
function and the conception of administration as basically
rule making be more absurd than in the recently expanded

area of welfare? In that area must be handled differentiated factors in successive individual cases far too numerous ever to be handled by courts and wholly beyond the competence of courts. If the job was to be given to the courts, they would have to become bureaucracies very much like those we have now.

The central fact is the shift in sovereigns, from royal to public. The sovereign will is no less to be served. The administrative search for morality is a search for appropriate ways to serve the popular will in action. Therefore, administrative theory needs to be seen, more than it has been formerly, as an aspect of political theory. Political theory, by the same token, should be less exclusively antecedent to rich experience in democracy, less legalistic, more full-bodied politically, and more related to administration. To point in that direction new arbitrary cross sections of government need to be made to facilitate various new analyses.

However unclear the distinction between the juridic and the executive functions and processes, it seems at least more illuminating and relevant now to search for it than to go on simply defining administration as the more specific formulation of the more general legislative formulations or to continue to build general administrative thinking around the favorite fictions of legal distinction, "quasi-legislative" and "quasi-judicial." These phrases assume a degree of reality in the separation of powers which would have overwhelmed us with governmental futility. They now are used to encourage rather thoughtless spreading of the process of one functional field over into other fields in special deference to small but powerful publics. They divert attention from the administrative reality and from fruitful pursuit of improved process in the executive field. For some years such effects have been extensive in the regulatory field.

REGULATORY ADMINISTRATION

It is a general purpose of government to establish a certain structure for the common life of its citizens. In some ways it is implicit in many of its activities that the structure so determined restrains citizens. Brigandage is restrained to make way for orderly commerce, certain processes are established to facilitate commerce, and so on, but these processes fix bounds as a means to facilitation. Just so does the ordering of language deprive a man of the ability to refer to a dog as a cat while it facilitates his capacity to communicate his meaning.

Many of the restraints of government are generally and indirectly felt, and some have very precise incidence with respect to particular actions and persons. One of the most ancient of governmental restraints has been accompanied by imprisonment, and another by some kind of ostracism or institutional containment of the ill or deranged. In these particular and tragic exercises of sovereignty concern for due process has been most common and most sustained before incarceration or segregation. Today as always the conduct of prisons and asylums is almost exclusively an administrative responsibility under legislative control. Yet it involves regulation at the point of concern ultimate for those regulated.

Other quite precise regulation characterized our government long before the establishment of the Interstate Commerce Commission is presumed to have introduced the regulatory function. The Customs Service, created by the fifth act of the first Congress, has provided regulations of commerce throughout our national history. Management of the public domain has regulated settlement and use of lands. The chartering of private banks as "national" banks long ago was associated with their regulation. Regulation through the postal service was stronger in earlier periods than now; in those years freedom of the press would not have been held to require automatic entitlement to a public subsidy, which was the point—not well made—in the *Esquire* case.

In modern development many laws of regulatory character are administered quite apart from the juridic orbit and with no demand for use of the juridic process. In earlier periods if a shipper of grain felt that his grain had been improperly graded to his disadvantage, he might, on a rare occasion, seek redress through the courts; with the establishment of governmental grain grading the process has become wholly executive. Meat inspection, executively handled, was imposed on packers shipping products in interstate commerce, but has been voluntarily sought by the largest packers with intrastate markets. Inspection of scales is another of many possible examples.

It has remained for a certain kind of administrative thinking and interest demand to concentrate attention on a small administrative area, to view this as the area of governmental regulation, and to impose in that area a procedure resembling a carbon copy of the juridic procedure. This effort was in the first instance more related to the great amount of revenues and investments involved than it was to the functions performed. The procedure indeed is one not readily useful to the ordinary citizen, even when for him the same issue may be relatively more important or when different concerns may relate more to primary human intrinsics. It may be worth asking whether this peculiar due process may not be, in some instances at least, a grant of special privilege.

The Interstate Commerce Commission provides the oldest example at the national level of an agency and a procedure so conceived. A principal consequence of its administrative organization and procedure has been a most complicated body of precedent and involved rationalization which even the most sophisticated find it all but impossible to unravel. Lawyers, who have largely patterned its processes, have not often attacked the Commission—at least for the reasons they give for attacking other regulatory agencies —but the Congress has demonstrated more than once by committee studies and by setting up special bodies to make other studies a considerable degree of dissatisfaction in behalf of important shipping publics, often geographical publics. The Commission's isolated status, associated with its administrative method, has made it largely immune to direct administrative intervention for purposes of reform, difficult for the Congress to relate to the points of its own dissatisfaction, and unco-ordinated with other governmental agencies having to do with transportation. For somewhat similar reasons the Hoover Commission expressed great dissatisfaction, as well as doubt about any important performance, in the case of the Federal Trade Commission. The point is that the required isolation and prescribed procedure may have minimized the public usefulness of the agencies.

The tendency in such cases was illustrated some years ago in the quite standard book by James Landis, *The Administrative Process*, which in spite of its title was addressed only to that small part of the administrative process which has been made juridic but has been carried on generally outside the courts. Landis first made a persuasive case showing why the courts could not handle such business, and then recommended the only administrative processes he knew—those which would make the regulatory agencies very closely resemble courts. He hardly dealt with administration at all in any other terms. Indeed, students in this field of executive regulation would be much put to it to find any items for a bibliography except books by lawyers having no knowledge of general administration, reports of committees of such lawyers, and decisions of courts and courtlike bodies.

Some eminent jurists have expressed penetrating insights now and again, but usually in the very broadest terms, so that most members of their profession either missed the point or were unable to carry it on to the area of application. Robinson's *Law and the Lawyers* was highly provocative but seems to have had little consequence relative to the present subject. The profession generally has ignored the vastly greater dimensions of nonregulatory administration and has not demonstrated any substantial recognition that there may be much to be learned about administration in those areas.

The dissent by Justice William O. Douglas in Cudahy Packing Co. *v.* Holland (315 U.S. 357, 1942) is in its specific language a notable exception among court opinions, reflecting insights deriving from outstanding administrative experience. The position expressed in that dissent later was made the position of the Supreme Court in Fleming *v.* Mohawk Wrecking and Lumber Co. (331 U.S. 111, 1947). In addresses and in books he has amplified his position, at one point referring to administrative agencies under democracy as "more and more the outposts of capitalism."

Judge Jerome Frank in various books has been most extensively penetrating in matters relevant to the present discussion. A brilliant student of political science, a highly successful private lawyer, a noted public administrator, and a United States Circuit Judge of great distinction, he has unequaled equipment for such studies. In *If Men Were Angels* he has made the point that regulatory commissions are more meticulous and laborious in their juridic procedures than the courts themselves. He says in explanation:

The Commission is far more afraid of possible censure by the upper courts than are the district judges on appeals from their decisions. The reversal of a trial judge is accepted as a routine matter; it never touches off an outcry for the abolition of the judicial system, nor for the repeal of the statute which the judge incorrectly construes. The reversal of an administrative order, however, often leads to charges of usurpation of power by the administrative agency, and to a demand for the destruction of that agency or of its statute. That judges are human and will therefore, not being capable of perfection, sometimes err is commonly taken for granted. But that common-sense attitude has not yet been widely accepted with reference to commissions.

A few pages farther on in the same book Frank makes another important point. Dealing with the field identified by Ruml, C. E. Merriam, and others as "private government," he emphasizes the fact that in effect much law delegates public powers to private institutions, notably corporations, and that the courts are more reluctant to intervene in the exercise of these powers than they are to restrain the government.

Those lawyers who attempt to create within the executive branch a separation of powers based on their "quasi-legislative" and "quasi-judicial" labels appear altogether reasonable to themselves. They have been wholly reasonable in their insistence that no one should judge his own case, that the same *members* within agencies should not act as prosecutor and also as judge. But the reality has not often been in conflict with these principles, and least often in the national levels where attorneys viewing it remotely have thought that violation of the principles was what they saw. The executive-administrative process is even harder to understand than the juridic, and the attorneys who would be contemptuous of laymen's discussion of courts, lawyers, and their ways should be quick to avoid tourist judgments of the general executive process. Efforts to hamper and traduce regulatory agencies in support of clients' short-term self-interest may easily inflict tragic long-term damage on the cause of private enterprise.

It is not intended to suggest that the executive-administrative process does not need critical attention or that the lax characteristics of lawyers' treatments of the subject are chiefly the fault of lawyers. The fault is with the practitioners and students of general public administration. There has been no formally developed, systematic theory of administration in terms different from, but somewhat comparable to, those of the juridic function and process. There are not even adequate *descriptions* of the administrative process. When these needed contributions are made, they may shed some light on the juridic, as well as on the executive, scene.

Process is important in both scenes, but the differences in time-learned practice suggest that process may require great differentiation. The basic term of reference is the governmental character—therefore, the political character—of both functional areas. Governmental character need not require a single kind of procedure, but in all areas it does require procedures consonant with their common political character. The tendency to deny this character is evident in both functional areas, reflecting the general ill regard for politics. Dealing just now only with this tendency in the juridic area, it seems worthwhile to cite in somewhat summary form a few of the generally important factors.

First perhaps is the peculiarly expert character, as distinguished from political character, now attributed to the courts and the status of the legal profession in the United States. The rise of the expert is a universal and important phenomenon and one posing increasing problems in all areas of public responsibility; yet in no democratic state so much as here have lawyers as a single expert body come to such dominance in all parts of government. Their *expertise* is often felt to cover all government. One entire branch of our government constitutes, in all terms except those of very remote control, a violation of the familiar dictum that experts should be on tap, not on top. In practice, only lawyers are eligible to that branch; to lawyers themselves is delegated the public responsibility of admitting to membership in their own body; in very general practice, only lawyers' nominations of other lawyers to court places are valid; only lawyers admit, and under sharp numerical limitations, students to law schools; and generally only lawyers (some of them brilliant and penetrating indeed) are accredited critics of lawyers and courts. Even as *expertise* relevance of this one competence to the modern technological-political reality is seriously to be questioned and sharply to be limited.

Second, the courts are not given the same kind or degree of scrutiny as is directed at executive and legislative branches. The judgment of lawyers about specific occupants of the bench passes generally in lieu of public judgment. In Washington, correspondents, Congress, and interest groups expend enormous energy trying to get behind the scenes in the executive area, and the correspondents are equally tireless concerning the legislature. The press prints on the whole ten times as much speculative news before the executive fact as it prints after the fact. To this the Supreme Court and all federal courts are substantially immune. News waits on the formal action, and freedom of the press is deemed real if only the decisions may be freely discussed—as of course they are, although with a dignity of discussion and a respectful tone not exactly common when the other branches are concerned. Lawyers generally comprise an especially powerful, vested-interest citizen group militantly supporting this special avoidance of scrutiny and criticism.

Third, the courts are by deliberate design and developed convention farthest removed from direct political and popular influence and control. While in many state and local jurisdictions the judges are elected, their nomination is often in special conventions to which only lawyers are thought to be fully eligible. The tendency also has been to fix relatively long terms, slowing the responsiveness of courts to popular changes, and to substitute appointments for elections. At the national level, of course, all judges of the central court system are life appointees, subject to impeachment in cases of extraordinary dereliction, and otherwise subject only to the restraints implicit in their process and to the self-restraint rooted in personal morality or desire for public approbation. Fortunately the courts have little power of initiative, and their case method, operating through precedent and judicial procedure, generally provides its own special restrictions. Such limitations make courts not only ill-qualified, but inappropriate, agencies of general administration. Reliance on such structural and procedural arrangements in the other branches would not be dreamed of by a vigilant and needful public.

Fourth, mention should be made of the almost unique contempt power residing in the courts. Even before recent developments giving it new importance it had constituted the most summary of powers, with nothing of a counterpart in the executive branch. During actual court proceedings it has had a very real justification and in modern practice in federal courts has been used only in that way. In other levels, too, it has come to be exercised with much restraint, but this is discretionary practice and not a part of a protective process. Excesses do appear, and they are not attacked with the vigor common in other criticisms of government. The first point here, however, is theoretical. No other branch of government directly checks this power; appeal is only within the hierarchy of courts. This exception to the general reliance upon checks and balances points up the very special removal of the courts from the general arena of popular government.

Under the Taft-Hartley Act this contempt power has reached a new phase in its development, being given new importance as an enforcement device in substitution for older means. It is questionable in that it eliminates juries. It is attractive in offering an effective way of dealing with corporations, an area to which older procedure has been ill-adapted. The new procedure may need much refinement.

Fifth, the rather exclusive reliance in juridic procedure on the debate technique removes it from the more political arena. The point is not the familiar one that debating is far from an ideal way to get at the whole truth, but rather that it calls for relatively simple, black-and-white decisions in each particular case, with shaded areas of decision appearing in time but at no particular time. This indeed is an admitted objective, making for relative clarity and stability in the area of the matters treated. Insofar as debating seems to be the method of political campaigns and legislative consideration there are two important differences: First, numerous debaters are engaged concurrently, resulting in complicated compromise and concurrent decisions by no means wholly consistent; and, second, the resulting decisions are broad and rather unclear general decisions related to the composition of majority, leaving room for further inconsistency and differentiation in administration distinguished by rather surprising flexibility in its search for acceptability.

Sixth, viewed institutionally the courts have little structure designed particularly to serve the basic political function of translating special interest into public policy. In the general hierarchy of legislative-executive government this is very much the essence of structure. Administrative appeal at successive hierarchal levels is at each level, not only to a broader responsibility than at the one below, but also to a point where the materials considered are somewhat automatically translated into terms of the broader responsibility. This is the function of hierarchy and co-ordination. In the courts, aside from the automatic difference in going from the state level to the national level by a break in hierarchy rather than by an organic continuation in hierarchy, reliance for the broader responsibility rests merely on an assumption of higher personal capacity. The prestige of the higher courts does in fact secure something of the sort assumed. But important organic elements are missing. In general organizational theory there would be no room for an assumption that hierarchy means nothing except higher personal capacity at each successive level. In executive-legislative hierarchy the terms of review must themselves be subtly translated as review progresses up the hierarchal ladder. In contrast, in the hierarchy of courts the lower courts seem to generalize more readily than the higher courts; certainly the Supreme Court goes to great lengths to pinpoint its decisions in avoidance of any possible general finding. In the circumstances, this appears to be a desirable and necessary evidence of restriction of the role of juridic process.

These factors of differentiation do not provide material for judgment of the performance of courts. They do serve to support the question whether the due process of the courts should be assumed to offer a pattern equally appropriate to administration outside of the courts where the materials and requirements are very different. They underscore the question whether attorneys, most often preoccupied with the problems of special, privileged clients, are likely to see executive due process in terms appropriate to the daily and diverse operations of popular government. These questions would challenge the wisdom of the Administrative Procedure Act of 1946, distinctly a product of the lawyers without benefit of administrators' advice. Making the hearing officer as administratively untouchable as a judge is only one of its transferences of juridic features to the administrative area. It may be argued that the best-administered regulatory activities were those carried on in regular executive departments rather than under independent boards and commissions, before the act of 1946 was put upon the books. Certainly the unco-ordinated isolation and rigidity of many of the strictly regulatory agencies have become serious handicaps to good government.

Perhaps there has been too much tendency to generalize about court procedure from a basis of too sweeping generalizations about the performance of courts. Even though we fully recognize the grave importance of the judiciary, we should reckon with the fact that not all courts or all court processes deserve sanctification. Local courts are generally partners in such governmental corruption as still is to be found in some of our cities. Perhaps they get no such share of graft as goes to executive malefactors, but the executive graft could not be so lush without a substantial bending of judicial rectitude in the area necessarily open to judicial discretion. If there is more bad government at the local level, there are by the same token more poor courts at that level and more formal and informal dominance of government by lawyers. This is the most ancient area of juridic functioning, where time should have brought much learning. It is also one of very special difficulty, of course, where the forces of lawlessness press hard and where most ordinary citizens appear at their weakest before the law. Police courts surely deserve more critical scrutiny than they are given.

Nonjudicial administration is closely associated with the judicial in the local, police area; and where the latter is bad the nonjudicial is worse. Local courts must share responsibility at this point of "law enforcement" where decisions are made to arrest a citizen or to seek an indictment. Bad examples might begin with a police practice in a college town of arresting students for offenses ignored in the case of permanent residents or of arresting Negroes for offenses ignored in the case of whites. Appalling examples of discrimination by the police courts in some northern cities find their sequel in actions by the police. The whole area explored by Raymond Moley in *Prosecution and Politics* deserves great public concern. It lies somewhat within the orbit of direct court influence and is an integral part of the "due process" so generally hallowed.

These areas of failing are not trivial. They are associated with local survivals of the political bad and a public failure to develop improved political structures and processes. But these items by no means tell the whole story, nor is it the purpose here to make any comprehensive judgment of the courts and their processes. Here it is intended only to suggest ways of looking critically at the record in order to question application of juridic thinking and process outside the juridic scene. In higher levels certainly and in all levels to a very heartening degree, the courts have been served with great devotion and ornamented by some very great minds and some very great spirits. A profound question is whether the effort to purify them of the political bad has moved or is moving them in any essential respects too far away from the political good, from popular service to service of special interests.

Perhaps the courts have been able to do generally so well because they could act generally so slowly. General administration clearly must have a faster tempo in dealing with, and responding to, felt need. Law is made for general administration, too.

Law for Administrators

Except when dealing specifically with the courts the primary purpose of legislatures in enacting law is to provide basis for administrative action. The principal determination is that there shall be action. This is an expression of sovereignty—popular sovereignty when the legislature is popular—calling for action in response to sovereignty. In a great many cases the action is not an umpiring of private differences, although it may be the administration of decisions in which the legislature already had acted as umpire. The umpiring role is more likely to have been between various interest groups than between individuals. But usually the interests umpired are so numerous and unlike that the process is not umpiring at all. Rather it is a process of distilling out of those various private interests something approximating the general interest. Making that general interest effective is the first task of administration.

Regarding law in this way, it becomes impossible to conceive of all citizens standing equal before the law except as they stand equal as political entities. Certainly the individual does not stand equal to the whole law, because he is not equal to the general public. The bar at which he has stood as an equal was in the polling booth or in the consideration of legislators. The right of the government to draft a youth for wartime service and the right of a mother to keep him at home cannot be treated as a difference between two equal litigants.

The "right" of popular government in such a case turns originally on feasibility. Feasibility is affected by urgency of the national need, but urgency determines acceptability, and acceptability is essential to feasibility. When conscription is less feasible it may be accompanied by a bonus for compliance or with allowance for the provision of a substitute. These were practices associated with enlistment in the Union forces at the time of the Civil War. When conscription was voted in World War I, it was believed to be more acceptable if administered through local citizen boards. Almost infinitely numerous variations in family and employ-ment situations then were handled by this semiformal, strictly executive kind of due process. The legislature strives for as high acceptability as possible in the form and timing of its enactment. In administrative application the responsi-bility is in part similarly to advance acceptability, which means, among other things, to advance some kind of adjust-ment to, and recognition of, the vast variation of family and employment situations.

Administration so realisitically visualized, as Dean W. A. R. Leys has pointed out in the *Public Administration Review*, is not merely the act of fixing a definite standard under a less definite standard laid down in law. If that were so, he says, administrative discretion would be the means of eliminating the need for administrative discretion in the future, whereas the responsibility and need for discretion continue. The ad-ministrators have to go on doing continually the same kind of weighing and measuring of values and acceptabilities the legislature itself had done already. Necessarily—and happily —good government is everywhere and in all its branches both "by law" and "by men."

Administering the law in its multiple forms and purposes is far more complicated business than existing literature, in its simplifying efforts, admits. Leys distinguishes three classes of discretionary powers: "(1) Technical discretion, which is freedom in prescribing the rule but not the criterion or end of action; (2) discretion in prescribing the rule of action and also in clarifying a *vague* criterion—this is the authorization of social planning; (3) discretion in prescribing the rule of action where the criterion of action is ambiguous because it is in dispute—this amounts to an instruction to the official to use his ingenuity in political mediation."

Leys was speaking in criticism of Ernst Freund's formula-tions and therefore used similar terminology. Any such use of "rule making," as already suggested, not only impedes comprehensive thinking about administration, but is often associated with an unhappy intrusion of legalistic ways into the conduct of administration. Forms written by attorneys —from the summons issued by a jury commissioner upward —often reflect an unnecessarily coercive rigidity and spirit and often fail to be sufficiently educational. In the same way, run-of-the-mill attorneys participating in dealings with citizens in behalf of executive agencies are notably bound by the rule-making spirit, therefore lacking in desirable imaginativeness and flexibility and on that account disproportionately responsible for public antagonism. Legal advertising is excessively legalistic and atrociously poor as advertising, meaningful at most to a small and special public.

Where administration directs the impact of the sovereign will upon citizens in causes not to be umpired, mere reliance on rule will deprive citizens of subtle resources in the considerateness made possible and induced by politics in popular government. At the same time the rule could so delay, make rigid, and confine the public interest as to deprive the public of its essential rights. It is both a necessity and a virtue that in a democratic, pluralistic society "public administration" should be a term hard to define, a process more subtle and variable than any set of administrative regulations can begin to suggest. In a memorable sentence Arthur Macmahon has described the reality as briefly as it can be put: "The problem of compulsion is lessened by the fact that the control methods of a moving consensus, although pinned initially by majority action at crucial points, will be largely a calculated interplay of inducements, incentives and indirect influences, not direct coercion."

In the general area of executive administration there exists in certain particulars the possibility of appeal to the courts, and in any particular the possibility of appeal to the legislature. Yet the obligation to citizens to provide a large part of the suitable process of government rests directly on the executive branch. It is an obligation not to be met with mere declarations that the existing processes are subtle and various. It must in manifold applications reasonably serve demands for equality, desert, human dignity, conscientious administration, and fulfillment of common expectations. These are terms used by Edmond Cahn in his philosophical consideration of the juridic process, *The Sense of Injustice*. They are terms bearing equally upon the legislative process, but the legislative process is not on that account to be a copy of the juridic. The terms bear fully upon the executive process. They represent the good, but they are not absolutes and are not absolutely right. Paraphrasing Cahn to fit the present purpose: "These are facets of good administration, ethical in nature; as they enter into the shaping of law and action they acquire a special direction and form qualified by the past history and the present felt need of the political-administrative system; so embodied, the ethical impulses must shrink to the size of their new responsibilities."

The courts and their present processes represent an accumulated learning of a specialized sort out of a long experience in a special area of public responsibility. But administrative agencies have their learning, too. It is not so far advanced perhaps as the learning of juridic institutions. Its scope is very much wider, and that which is to be learned steadily piles high the task. What has been learned is not much recorded in books. But a good deal has been learned, and the principal repository of this learning is in the administrative institutions and processes. They have been under very much more severe pounding from time and public than the courts, and whatever the quality of their learning, it has been acquired in its own environment in the course of carrying on the functions of that area of government. These politically responsible agencies have been adjusting steadily to expressions of a sense of injustice not restrained as are the comments concerning courts. Criticisms require attention, but attention should include some understanding of the processes as they are. The formulas of reform devised in, and growing out of, another area of government may not be the best of all possible proposals.

The cornerstone of due process is not in the courts, enormously important as they are. The colonies along our Atlantic seaboard in the second half of the eighteenth century simplified their demand for the basic process into a slogan: "Taxation without representation is tyranny." The cornerstone of due process, in other words, is laid in the politics of popular control of representative government. In the executive field, perhaps there is no phrase but "good administration" to identify the values sought.

V

ADMINISTRATION, COURTS, AND LEGISLATURES

DEMOCRATIC government must be both responsive and responsible. The first need of operating democracy is to achieve response to a public sense of some particular disorder. The second need is to fix and identify officials whom the public may hold accountable for the response as it has been governmentally formulated. The third is the need to differentiate within the ordered unity brought about in response to public need, deferring to the pluralistic character of democratic unity. The first is the enduring problem of *e pluribus unum*. The third is the problem of *ad plura unum*. These two are together the problem of responsiveness. The second is the peculiar problem of responsibility.

Under public determination we have no problem of centralization *versus* decentralization; we have a continuing problem of centralization *and* decentralization. Responsiveness in truly public terms cannot be ensured without adequate organs of unity. The response cannot be differentially carried into action without subordinate agencies of differentiation; these must provide the values intended when "decentralization" is invoked. Decentralization of that which is not centralized is a conception involving misuse of organizational terms with reference to something not organized. All three branches of the government are agencies of both centralization and decentralization. All are centers of response to public need, especially charged with the duty of devising responses flexible and various in different applications. They are centers of responsibility, together responsible to each other and separately responsible to the public. Without such centers democratic government could have no real meaning. Centers of responsibility, they are citadels of leadership.

REPRESENTATIVE LEADERSHIP

Throughout these pages we shall be considering responsibility, but at this point we wish only to identify it as associated with leadership having a representative character. In a complex and numerous society all but the most intimate of one's concerns must be directed toward individuals made institutionally, formally or informally, representative of those concerns. The representative function is almost a universal, so necessary that some are inclined to argue that democracy is never real or truly feasible—failing to see that democracy inevitably determines the kinds of representativeness and thereby attains its great significance. Almost nothing in systematic literature deals directly with the phenomenon of representation, but here, too, we must proceed by merely noting the distinctly representative character of responsible political leadership and then considering the discretion and controllability of that leadership. Because leadership is representative in a complicated, institutional way, the approach to responsible public administration begins with consideration of crucial leadership in a pattern of control.

Basic assumptions in the present discussion are three: First, that public administration participates importantly in policy making; second, that the policies and actions of government are the product of the *effective* political sentiment of the time and place; third, that the morality of government is a product of the effective moral sentiment of the time and place.

What sentiments out of all existing sentiments are effective is determined by the form and character of political institutions and arrangements which are the vehicles of sentiments. The pattern of control extends through all of these institutions and arrangements, whose variety makes for complicated and pluralistic control.

In all of these institutions and arrangements facilities for leadership exist, and leadership operates as a special factor of influence on sentiment, helping to create, to form (to confer organization upon), and to determine what sentiments are effective. That the role of leadership is limited in all societies and states was recognized by so dominant a figure as Bismarck in his remark previously quoted defining politics as "the art of the possible." In democracy a slight but significant twist may be given to that definition by making it "the art of the satisfactory." The limits on leadership are everywhere the limits beyond which the effective public will not assent, be persuaded, or be influenced. In popular government the effective public is a wide public, and assent assumes a content of higher as well as broader willingness.

Leadership roles, then, are exercised in influencing, identifying, and operating within, respective areas of discretion. While such areas of discretion widen and contract with particular leaders and with changes in time and circumstance, they are always confined within limits policed by the public and somewhat roughly made clear by history, institutions, and custom.

Administrative areas of discretion are generally—with some particular exceptions with respect to some functions for a few institutional chief executives in certain jurisdictions—narrower than the areas of discretion available to legislatures. Individual members of legislatures, being less responsible and more various than the body as a whole entity, may range fairly widely and experimentally if only they narrow their range of discretion where it bears directly upon their individual constituencies; this range of individual legislators depends, however, upon established practices of responsibility to party. Individual political leaders actually in office may range in advocacy more widely than the legislature ranges in action as a body, and less widely than the range of advocacy covered by individual legislators. Political leaders out of office but in places of major responsibility in a party out of power are limited less than those of the party in power. Those courting third-party clienteles may range far.

Altogether, the exercise of discretion in the ranges indicated is the means by which out of many conceivable variations in direction and form of policy and action the few which are really within the range of possibility are identified, and choice then progressively narrowed. While citizen discussion may seem to imply many more possibilities, few of the ideas discussed are really a feasible majority position at a particular time in the circumstances of that time, and it is a primary role of leadership to formulate and identify those few. Even in very crucial and complicated matters, perhaps a half-dozen possibilities is a normal maximum of the feasible, and often only two or three may be discerned. Very often the exercise of discretion has to do with slight modifications and shifts with reference to a single program to which no alternative has come within the range of the possible. These slight modifications have great importance, of course; in successive decisions they may effect a marked change in course to something not earlier apparent as an alternative, or they may bring us back to a position from which deviation had occurred. Since the possible positions are few, not all the discussion conceivable is necessary to identify and explore those positions.

This whole picture is one of gradually narrowing the range of discretion according to degree of responsibility for decision, but concentrating on that narrower area of responsibility the dynamism of the whole relevant process of agitation, proposal, and pursuit of popular appeal. The whole process is a search for more satisfactory government. As a facet of this indicative of political health, it is worth noting that in the United States there is a recognized responsibility for leadership to strive to elevate the governmental practice in terms of distinctly moral character. In various ways the public expects leadership to try to achieve in government higher standards than exist generally in organized private society. This is particularly true with respect to the national government. We do all seem readier to suffer mediocrity gladly—or even to insist upon it—among our familiars than among those distant. But it would be reasonable to assume that this higher demand on the national government is associated with the fact that we see the mediocrity around us as the necessary condition of the rank and file, and exact proportionately more of each level of eminence, leadership, and responsibility. Certainly we do expect the national government to set a particularly high standard in its treatment of employees, in the quality of its personnel, in the quality of its governmental performance. We especially like to see the national governmental buildings have dignity and a certain monumental character. We wish the national capital to be an especially beautiful city, and we visit it in a citizen-tourist stream which gives stirring evidence of an aspiring patriotism higher and deeper than any parochial pride. And while we readily accept the private practice of cutting friends in on an especially profitable operation, we quickly denounce any national official who seems to practice personal favoritism.

The moral dynamism of our democracy as evidenced in

many ways thus supports our reliance upon the public as the final determinant of our moral fate. We may believe that the citizen under democracy is freer to be moral in his exactions of government than he is in his private affairs, or that the reliance of government on its citizens induces continuing elevation of these exactions, putting ever higher premiums on, and establishing new interpretations of, equity, equality of opportunity, and general welfare. These new interpretations are only incidentially and in a restricted way, however importantly, related to the processes of courts; they emerge in political process and penetrate all government. The processes of politics also gradually confer design upon the pattern of control, concentrating ever more narrowly but variously on responsible officials. It is this concentration that is crucial to responsibility. Among officials, the most representative in character and function are the most important to the morality of government; in them should be the essential centralization of power and responsibility.

Various views of government involve differences in judgment about what is essential centralization of power and responsibility. Common fear of government often tends to support irresponsible and uncontrollable government by seeking too much dispersal of power and responsibility. Any federal system poses a special difficulty, too, making responsibility very often a matter of uncertainty. But in general it is submitted that such centralization is necessary as will permit the public to get done through government what it seeks to do through government and to identify responsibility for its conduct so that the public may enforce correction and change. There must be enough centralization to provide identifiable officials with the power to intervene with respect to anything in government on which the public demands intervention. Given that centralization, a very great deal of decentralization becomes feasible and desirable, and it may be effected through many administrative forms, only one of which is the use of states in the "grant-in-aid" form. The public itself, assured of the power to intervene, will willingly refrain, or be persuaded to refrain, from intervention on many technical and difficult matters. It may, and it does, issue a particular ordinance of self-denial by deferring its right of speedy intervention in some areas, such as those assigned to the courts. Those areas are restricted, as befits territory occupied by officials of a very special sort lacking in representative character.

The pattern of popular control, then, concentrates responsibility in leadership in the three branches of government. Administration, to be responsible, must tie appropriately to those three headships.

THE NATIONAL LEVEL

In its relationship to the courts the executive branch of government may not differ essentially from private citizens and corporations. It recognizes a certain organic kinship to the judicial branch, an intimate association with it, and a somewhat constant involvement in past court decisions and possibility of judicial review. Its business is conducted with ready legal advice in terms, among others, of that involvement. But the discipline of this relationship and that legal review is so routinized as to loom, for most administrative areas and most administrators, relatively no larger than looms the chance of arrest or "trouble with the government" for most citizens.

In spite of common talk about regimentation most citizens go their ways feeling so familiar with governmental disciplines, and those disciplines so much a matter of climate and habit, that they have little consciousness of the disciplines in the wide play of daily discretion. Citizens labor on their taxes with groans, get their various licenses, encounter traffic policemen, but otherwise are not on the average much involved in actual dealings with the government. Yet all the while they act according to general patterns considerably affected by government. Most of their talk about regimentation is directed against the national government, although for most citizens contact with the government is much more at state and local levels, which are no less governmental. Only persons and organizations with large affairs are extensively and constantly involved with the national government or with government altogether, and for most of those the relationship becomes a matter of systematic organizational handling and advice of counsel.

So it is in the executive branch with relation to the judicial. Things are done in a climate considerably affected by the judiciary. Some executive officials have much to do with the strictly legal aspects of the business, and there are relatively large legal staffs engaged in consultation and review. Everything that is done is done with no lack of regard for, or willing sensitivity to, the courts and their findings. No one wishes to be responsible for, or to receive, a court spanking or to open a breach that would bring criticism. But most of the interpretation of law is carried on so far within the limits of legal propriety that most administrators interpret the law as citizens generally do; for themselves, with no danger of embarrassment, and for the most part without even being conscious that they are interpreting the law. The exercise of discretion taxes each official's capacity without often taxing the boundaries of the legal, and still less frequently impinging upon the area within judicial responsibility.

These things are true in considerable part because the Supreme Court functions, as they have been clarified through the years, have been chiefly two. One of these is defense, enforcement, and interpretation of civil rights. The other is the adjudication of federal and state powers. Looking at the whole area of public administration, it is clear that the bearing of the Court on it is much limited.

The civil-rights function has been generally clarified as chiefly serving to keep open the basic processes of democratic politics. These basic processes are chiefly those of individual expression rather than those relating to the organization and performance of political institutions, such as parties; they have to do with free speech and assembly, the rights of dissent, the separation of church and state, the avoidance of discrimination. These important concerns do not take an acute form covering any large part of the executive field. In this area the general political climate and the capacity for political control of the government make for a habitual practice well reflective of established standards. It is a rare case where civil rights can be directly and clearly raised in executive administration. Where the effort has been made, the Court has drawn a wavering course of intervention seeking to ensure absence of discrimination. This has touched a very small part of the whole administrative area, has usually turned upon some special and limited notion of due process, and often has tended actually to be discriminatory by requiring special procedure in behalf of a few special interests. Some of the rare cases have been constructively important, however, actually protecting political vitality; often these have applied especially to local government. In this whole function the Court enthrones political science rather than law in its usual practitioner terms, and performs least well when its reasoning is heavily legalistic.

The second primary function of the Court, the adjudication of federal and state powers, is one of critical usefulness in our system. Here, however, the direct impact is most often upon law itself, not so often directly upon administration. Court decisions in this field have been important in determining a good deal of our pattern of inducement and

co-operation, and, therefore, the general administrative shape
of many programs. This has complicated administration and
confused responsibility at the same time it has developed
some peculiar values in American government. But the impact of this function upon administration has been chiefly
through the legislature.

All this is not to say that the structure of law as it bears
upon administration as a whole is simple or easy. Perhaps no
single action taken by an official is governed by just a single
law, however complicated the one law may be. A good many
laws bear upon the whole government, and a good many
different laws bear particularly upon any special part or
function of the government. Any new enactment cannot be
considered by itself, but only in association with all the other
prior laws that bear upon the same persons, organizations,
functions, and situations. And, of course, the strictly legal
documentation developed within the course of administration is enormous, even though a very small fraction of the
whole documentation. In certain areas of government, as in
the regulatory area, the strictly legal preoccupations and determinants have a much greater frequency. But for administration in general, any such preoccupation with the legalistic aspects as some observers expect would be impossible
and undesirable. Good administration, like good citizenship,
has no such necessity.

For many administrative fields there are literally no court
decisions that are any more applicable than they would be
to any citizen. For areas where court decisions have more
direct bearing, the number of decisions is extremely small in
proportion to the volume of transactions handled administratively, and their coverage of the whole content of those
transactions is much smaller still. A few decisions reflecting
judicial efforts to impose on the executive branch an inappropriate process determine unhappily a pattern of process

for certain kinds of transactions. More often, particular court decisions mark certain boundary points of the area of discretion available to administrators and thereby have a general effect, quickly achieved, soon habitual and before long hardly in the area of consciousness. For the most part the existence of the courts is a somewhat vague background factor of rather general, pervasive but reserved, effect. The courts probably have a relatively more constant impingement on the legislature.

The general administrative concern with law is immeasurably more oriented to the legislature than to the courts; for the legislature can and does affect the administrator and his problems much more directly, variously, and constantly. In the national government, the administrative concern with "the intent of Congress" is never ending. The concern is not limited to the intent of a single enactment or to actual enactments altogether. It is a concern with the power to enact, the possibility of enactment. Even more, it is a concern with the limiting opinions and attitudes of particular congressional committees, particular committee chairmen, and individual members of Congress rather generally. Any particular member of Congress can make life dreadful for anyone with respect to almost anything done administratively. No such pervasively penetrating concern on the part of individual administrators with respect to individual legislators is to be found in any other democratic government.

This detailed influence of splintered segments of the legislature presents some peculiar problems in governmental morality. Generally it would be felt to have moral value for the executive branch and individual administrators to draw close to the legislative branch to improve communication between them. Yet intimacy between individuals in the two branches leads to expectations of special influence on the part of the individual legislators; and for the administrator to subject himself to special influence, even on the part of a legislator, is to begin the granting of special favors which is soon a corruption of government. This is particularly true, as a rule, in relationships with younger members of the legislature; the longer experienced usually grow in responsibility and perspective and are more skilled in sifting out of the special demands made upon them those that have general significance for the public interest or that contribute to operating equity.

Concern for improved communication between the two branches has led some agencies to, and other agencies to consideration of, the establishment of agency offices in congressional office buildings. The thought was to select some official thoroughly acquainted with the work of the agency and to have him readily available as a source of information for members of Congress. There would be very few persons so generally informed, and the very assignment of one would prevent him from continuing to be thoroughly acquainted with the work of his agency; he would be moved out of the flow of that work, and his personal information would become quickly out of date. More important, agencies engaging in this practice found their representatives to become quickly divested of the function of supplying information to congressmen, and vested with the function of prosecuting administrative requests coming from particular members of Congress.

The general tendency in the executive branch is to respond readily to the legislature. This inclination extends even to individual legislators in every concession not clearly in violation of good practice. Willingness to defer to the individual legislators is highest as a general thing in agencies not themselves exposed widely to the public. Having little confidence in its own political competence and having actually less basis for knowing the popular scene, such an agency tends to yield without too much discrimination to the admitted and basic power of the legislature. (The case of former Congressman Andrew Jackson May grew out of such administrative yielding.) On the other hand, an agency deeply involved in daily business with a large public develops its political responsibility and competence along more complicated lines, and on occasion will resist individual legislators or legislative committees more strongly.

There is a distinction, of course, between the proper exercise of influence or control by the legislative body and the exercise of influence or control by an individual member or committee of that body. Control by the legislative body over administration is basically real and unquestioned, but beyond this is a strong and general inclination to defer to legislative members. Many times, indeed, the request of a member deserves compliance as essential to his role as a member. In general, for example, any member is entitled to all the information he may seek, and in general he is honestly given it even though difficulty of communication sometimes leaves the information unsatisfactory. Very rarely there may occur cases of willful misleading; this writer recalls one such case, which resulted in the discharge of the guilty official.

There are many practical problems involved, however, even in so apparently simple a rule as the one requiring the giving of full information. A common request, particularly during an election year, is for lists of employees living in a particular state or congressional district. Hundreds of these requests may come in a short period to a single agency having tens of thousands of employees altogether. Each of the requests in one or more particulars will differ from all the others; each request will entail a great deal of work; and some of the details sought may not be a matter of record at all, while some other details, although of record, are of a sort not regularly tabulated and therefore are deeply buried in individual personnel records. It may be believed that some particular items requested are rather incidental and accidental, depending upon just how it occurred to the congressman to formulate his inquiry. Tens, or even hundreds, of thousands of dollars of extra cost might be involved in answering specific inquiries in precisely the terms in which they were made. Apparent reluctance to give precise reply may be suspiciously pounced upon, yet it is altogether likely that a tabulation of information readily available will serve the congressman's purpose reasonably well. In such cases letters of explanation reflecting willingness to reply precisely if that is indeed necessary usually result in ready acceptance of the easily available. Where such requests are poorly handled, ill will and suspicion are fanned.

This problem of precise replies to requests for information extends beyond the legislative area, of course. Chief Justice Arthur T. Vanderbilt of the New Jersey Supreme Court tells frequently in speeches of an unhappy experience. He had wired to a federal agency to ask the number of checks issued by it in the course of a good many years, and the total amount of money involved. The amount of money would have been easy, but the number of checks had never before been regarded by anybody as important information, and it was information not developed in the course of operations. After the fact, getting that information would have been very costly. The request of the judge appeared just as silly to the agency as his experience with the agency seemed silly to him. But his request was handled very unimaginatively—slowly, reluctantly, and without explanation of administrative difficulty.

As between the executive branch and the legislative there are a few requests for information that are difficult for other and more serious reasons. Files developed in the course of personnel investigations are one example. Those files characteristically contain reports of interviews with citizens who would consent to frank speech only on the condition that their remarks be treated as strictly confidential and private. A request from the legislature or from legislators for such files raises questions of conflicts in moral responsibilities to legislature and citizen. There is also the question of making public such information as may reflect upon some employee or former employee in ways not supported by all available information. Legislators have been known to use such materials in most unjust ways. Such requests, therefore, raise questions that have sometimes to be treated in terms of the equality of powers in co-ordinate branches of the government. Questions of this order occur only once in hundreds of thousands of requests for information. Where the decision is not to respond, it is never made by any official ranking below the head of an agency, and usually then only after consultation with the Attorney General and the President. In cases where the Congress would feel sincerely affronted, the refusal will be made only by the President. The issue is raised more frequently in the areas of foreign policy and military security than in any others. Usually, in some informal way sufficient information is made avilable to especially responsible members of Congress, so that there is no real sense of denial. Even with respect to personnel investigations, individual members of Congress often will be permitted informally to read the moot material or to listen to its reading with names of informants omitted and under conditions making actual recording of the information impossible.

In general, information flows from the bureaucracy to the legislative branch with the greatest freedom, constancy, and multiplicity of source. In general, too, the mature members of the legislative branch are satisfied about these relationships.

The absence of general and supported complaint from these seasoned members is significant. The chorus of wholesale complaint comes usually from younger members, to be joined in by their elders only occasionally in the tactics of particular situations. The overriding situation is one of general legislative rivalry and party opposition to the chief executive, supported by the complexity and dimensions of their mutual business. The rivalry flows from the separation of powers, and the party of opposition is implicit in the two-party system. Some of the rivalries are aspects of the pattern of responsibility more or less peculiar to the United States. Evidences of their being should not be confused with evidences of either legislative or executive irresponsibility.

Perfecting the relationship between executive and legislative *branches* turns upon manner and method of legislative review, and the burden of improvement in these falls first upon the legislature in its need to become equal to its modern task. This is not to suggest that the efficiency of Congress is something to be measured with tools of "scientific management." In a large way the efficiency of Congress as a public agent is very high. Its function is not expert but politically representative. Congress stands between all the specialized functions and the still more specialized bodies of experts engaged within the functional agencies on the one hand, and the public on the other hand. The effort to make Congress itself expert is, of all reform proposals, the most unconsciously subversive of popular government. It would stall government in continuing warfare between two bureaucracies; much worse, it would substantially deprive the public of crucially important representatives.

The essence of the pattern of popular control is in the successive subordinations of the more special interest and function to the more general. Each such subordination must exist in terms of each level upward within the executive hierarchy and in terms of the whole executive hierarchy as situated next under the legislative level. In the progression upward in the executive hierarchy there is an inevitable movement away from *expertise* to functional preoccupation appearing as specialization, to ever broader and more general interests and responsibilities. The cabinet members are not experts, the President is not expert; still less should Congress be expert.

The present efficiency of Congress is achieved at high cost to the members of Congress, just as the efficiency of some executives is achieved at the high cost of extraordinary hours and effort. The problem of Congress is to learn how to operate more consistently at the proper level of Congress so as to treat, for the public and in terms of the whole public interest, with major matters of paramount concern to the public.

Sophisticated members of Congress recognize this need in private expressions regarding the tendency to deal most in unmanageable particulars and least with general determinations. This tendency gives rise to numberless fishing inquiries which tend to make the general appear to turn too much on matters most particularistic. It is associated with the manner of the opposition party, on the whole rather peculiar to this government, a manner of extravagant criticism which keeps the public unnecessarily alarmed and diverts public attention from matters of most intrinsic moment. These failings in large part reflect a sense of congressional insecurity. The practice, in a vicious circle, aggravates that sense of insecurity.

The importance of Congress is profoundly real. If it could act in that confidence, strong in its public function, it would see itself as the level of government generally next higher than the executive, and would reserve to itself a function of review substantially resembling that of the next higher level in a hierarchy conceived in executive terms. The level below could then intelligently present the very issues that had taxed its own discretion and existing authorities. In this interchange whatever could not be explained in terms meaningful and acceptable to the more general view and responsibility would not be accepted. And there would be confidence that what Congress would find acceptable, the public would find acceptable. For Congress to attempt to pass upon the special in expert terms is inappropriate, duplicatory, unconstructive, and weak.

Maintenance of review appropriate to its level would simplify and improve generally the functional relationships between executive and legislative. It would clarify many of the relationships between President and Congress, including those between the Budget Bureau and Congress. But the relationships at the presidential level have peculiar aspects that are for later and special attention. What has been discussed here is the general relationship of legislature and bureaucracy, and here it can only be affirmed that the intervention of the President between the bureaucracy and the Congress is a crucial feature of our system, constituting a very special and important element in the pattern of popular control.

STATE AND LOCAL

This discussion of relationships between the executive, the judiciary, and the legislature has been couched principally in terms of the national government. There are, of course, many differences at the state and local levels. Differences exist as between the very numerous jurisdictions, and as between functions.

At the local level, for example, the great relative difference in the percentage of the area of government occupied by law enforcement increases the relative importance of the bearing of the courts upon administration.

In both state and local governments the relative infrequency of legislative sittings and absence of full-time responsibility of legislators make for less constant and pervasive legislative influence and control. At the local level rather generally, and in some states where civil service has not erected high barriers, these factors are associated with a relatively high frequency and completeness of control of specific administrative actions by individual members of the legislative bodies in personal and/or political capacities. This results in an exercise of power disproportionate and inappropriate to the responsibility of legislative membership.

Because of the relatively great number of elective posts in most states and localities, the pattern of control is still more ill-defined, responsibility still more unclear. "Cabinet members" are often quite independent of the official who is nominally "chief executive." In many states the representational pattern is badly distorted. In counties and municipalities, ward and district structure provide facilities for the special interest and minimize over-all popular responsibility. Other constitutional, legal, and charter arrangements contribute even more confusion in various ways in various jurisdictions. There are important differences also in varying developments and uses of party responsibility. In Connecticut, for example, the governor has insignificant control of the executive establishment, and the legislature generally votes according to a strict party division. In California the practice of dual filing in party primaries diminishes party responsibility to the vanishing point. Franchise limitations and state and local one-party situations have their first and probably their greatest adverse significance at state and local levels. All of these things confuse and diminish administrative responsibility and dilute the popular character of control.

They all bear upon the role and character of legislative review of administration, and many of them bear also upon the responsibility of the chief executive, next to be discussed.

Grants-in-aid from state governments and from the national government to state and local levels provide an important example of the governmental higher level's capacity to attain and to impose higher standards than would be spontaneously and soon attained by the lower levels. These standards tend to radiate an elevating influence into fields not directly affected. Where actually imposed, they reflect administrative responsibility to the highest legislative level involved. There is at the same time, as studies conducted by William Anderson at the University of Minnesota disclose, a contradictory result, confusing political responsibilities. The studies were expected to disclose most often and most significantly clashes in governmental "sovereignties." Instead, they unfolded chiefly a picture of growing functional sovereignties, tending to combine workers in particular kinds of activities, regardless of the levels of government by which they were employed, in loyalty to program, and in that loyalty tending to circumvent political control at any and all levels.

The whole city-manager movement is much more significant than the simple provision of professional managers. It has been accompanied by a clarification of responsibilities, diminishing petty legislator interference and at the same time elevating fundamental legislative control and consolidating executive responsibility. The conscious avoidance by professional managers of any pursuit of tenure rights has been itself a high attainment of governmental morality.

The extension of civil service in many state governments and increasingly in the cities has contributed to elevation of the level of legislative review and control. The development of staff officers as supporting chief executive responsibilities, improved budgeting, and the diversification of activities have also helped to put state and local governmental arrangements of responsibility well ahead of conditions obtaining a decade or two ago.

These are, of course, merely illustrative of many governmental improvements at state and local levels, in spite of their particular difficulties. The New York State government is outstanding in its general development and in concentration of responsibility on its chief executive. The frequency with which the governor and legislature represent opposing parties suggests need for representational reform which would make for truer popular control and improved legislative review. Under the governor, however, executive responsibility is extraordinarily vivid in that state.

The general picture is one showing clearest development of the patterns of responsibility and popular control at the level of the national government, on which there have been long and great concentrations of public attention, criticism, and expectation. At that level we find generally the greatest refinement of administration associated with the clearest patterns of responsibility. Even the imperfections in the representativeness of the Congress derive very largely from intrastate political arrangements.

VI

EXECUTIVE RESPONSIBILITY

Large powers and unhampered discretion seem to me the indispensable conditions of responsibility. Public attention must be easily directed, in each case of good or bad administration, to just the man deserving of praise or blame. There is no danger in power if only it be not irresponsible. If it be divided, dealt out in shares to many, it is obscured; if it be obscured, it is made irresponsible.

Woodrow Wilson, THE STUDY OF ADMINISTRATION

Public opinion is impotent so long as it allows itself to be kept guessing which shell the pea is under, whether the accountability is with the foreman, or the local manager, or the general manager or the directors.

E. A. ROSS, SIN AND SOCIETY

LARGE powers are necessary to a large and powerful nation. Powers must be divided into parts, dealt out in shares to many—as Wilson knew well. The parts require integration. The key to the morality that is rooted in responsibility is in not permitting ourselves to be kept guessing which shell the pea is under.

The two feasible focuses of responsibility under popular government are the legislature and the *chief* executive. Under the system peculiar to the United States, characterized by federalism, separation of powers, and weak parties, the power potential is dissipated, diffused, and confused; but here, too, whatever concentration of public power is possible comes into focus at these two points. When in doubt the general public can look with justifiable hope of satisfaction no further than to these two central repositories of responsibility. They not only symbolize, they do in fact constitute, all of the centralizing necessity and reality of responsibility that we have achieved. If by citizen demands they are unaffected, at least to the point of institutional response, the concern that moves the citizen must be regarded as something less than a concern of the public as at the time constituted.

These two centers of power are organically attuned through politics to public sentiment. While both delegate powers largely and cannot in the first instance be responsible for everything that is done, whatever delegations they may have made of whatever power they have can be withdrawn, and actions under the delegations modified, reversed, compensated. The continuing reality of such review and change is a fundamentally important aspect of the day-to-day business of popular government. The capacity for such review and change is a pervasive governor of administration in dimensions far greater than the dimensions of the innumerable post-factum instances of it. This capacity shapes action in the first place, and constantly induces change and rectification at administrative levels far below conscious attention at the centers of power.

The presidency—and to varying degrees the chief-executive pattern in the various jurisdictions of the other levels of American government—is an institution unique in the history of governance. While power is much more centered in the Prime Minister in British-type governments than is commonly realized, it is centered somewhat less in him than the lesser executive power available to the American government is centered in the President. This relatively slight difference is not the principal one, however. The chief distinction of the presidency is that it is in an extraordinary way the special agency of the whole public.

Under the British practice members of Parliament are elected without much relationship to their places of residence. While chosen by particular constituencies, they have a more general derivation and responsibility than is characteristic of our members of Congress. The Prime Minister as a member of Parliament is chosen by a single constituency and by his party, not by nationwide suffrage. In Britain speculation about "the next Prime Minister" is speculation concerning a determination "they" will make, and "they" are strangely and variously described as king, the outgoing Prime Minister and the somewhat indefinite "party leadership." In contrast, speculation about the next President here is speculation concerning highly popular processes. In Britain responsibility is very much more in party. It is probably more in party there with a relatively homogeneous, smaller, less volatile people than our highly pluralistic and far-flung population ever would permit or find satisfactory here. The President as an individual is the one peculiar creature of our pluralistic complexity, and he plays a role essential to our tenuous and difficult unity. As compared with a Prime Minister, whose strength may be chiefly intraorganizational with party leaders and Parliament, the President draws his strength more directly from the general public.

The pattern of popular responsibility centers, then, in President and Congress, and between them. From the President, lines in the pattern run to his party generally, somewhat particularly to those somewhat special factors of party that are involved in presidential nominating conventions, and outward to the whole public. On another side, the pattern runs on various bright threads of power control from the President through the entire executive bureaucracy and from the parts of that bureaucracy again outward to the whole public and to many publics. On another side, the lines run between President and Congress, through Congress, and once more outward to the public. On still another side, the lines run between bureaucracy and Congress and again outward from both to the public.

PRESIDENT AND CONGRESS

The President has a role of legislative leadership related to, but to a degree distinguishable from, his role of chief executive. He has a function of general public leadership similarly related to his executive nature and somewhat distinguishable from it in ceremonial and some other particulars. Here we concentrate attention on his relations with Congress as they bear upon his chief-executive functions.

This is an area of inescapable difficulty. The theory of the separation of powers provides fundamental handicaps to organizational unity, however incomplete the separation may be in both the Constitution and the operating reality. To an important degree we have a structure of co-ordinates who in various ways are not at all equal. In many respects (most of the time in most respects) Congress as a body is the superior in actual power possessed. Yet even in connections in which this is true and when the power actually exercised is predominantly congressional, many citizens and members of Congress do not readily understand that it is true. This misunderstanding is common when Congress gives approval to a proposal originating within the executive branch. The approval is not mandatory, as Congress has demonstrated on innumerable occasions, but there is a tendency to feel that in concurrence power has been relinquished. Sometimes the inclination is to engage in a wasteful search for ways to withhold agreement and consciously to impose congressional power. This is but one example of the general fact of rivalry implicit in a difference in functions and particularly implicit in a formal separation of powers. Another and very important factor affecting the relationship is the dissipation of congressional power within its own parts.

In some respects the President is the more powerful. Some basis for attributing superiority to him lies in his special responsibility for foreign policy, but insofar as this is a power of mere initiation it is an unreal superiority. Treaties must have two-thirds support in the Senate, and other negotiations increasingly are becoming subject to organic authorizing legislation and specific appropriations. In general, and more truly now than in earlier periods, the President is much dependent on the Congress in the foreign field. Even greater limitations on his power in this field are erected by foreign governments of course. Perhaps only on extraordinary occasions and in the important policy associated with military action as commander in chief is he at all clearly independent of, or superior to, Congress.

Indeed, with respect to Congress the President has influence rather than power. The resemblance of his influence to power is perhaps related to the fact that he is one and dramatic, while members of Congress are many and usually dramatic only individually. It is much easier for the President to formulate and propose one thing, at the point of his relationship to Congress, than it is for Congress to consolidate its force upon a single alternative. As the one executive head and as the one official elected by the whole nation, his influence is more pointed and concentrated.

Nevertheless, the President is intricately and thoroughly dependent upon Congress, and the conduct of the relationship is very important both to him and to Congress in their common responsibility. For the relationship, the burden rests most on the President, and it is most difficult for him to carry it for the very reason that concentrates his influence:

he is one, and the members of Congress sensitive to the relationship are 531. All concerned have many other relationships, and with the best of will and sustained effort this particular relationship will always be less than fully satisfactory.

In an organization of normal structure, such a relationship would be based on hierarchy, and to some extent it is here. Normally, too, that hierarchy in Congress would be predicated on party responsibility, with the President clearly at the apex of the party hierarchy. But in the United States, party is peculiarly undisciplined and organized only in skeletal terms. In consequence the congressional members of the President's own party tend to be organizational mavericks and require attention in terms of their high individualism. Dealing with the Vice-President, who is always an independent political leader in his own right, with the President pro tem of the Senate, and with the Speaker, the two party leaders, and two party whips does not suffice. Not even this group can be counted upon as a unity; they must be individually courted, and important attentions, concessions, and favors must be bestowed upon them individually and upon the group. The job is then only begun, and even that beginning is never ended.

The general result is that not only new policies but the whole conduct of the executive branch are eternally dependent upon the judgment and many favorable actions on the part of Congress as a body and its membership in considerably individualized terms. From this dealing flow many influences altering the way of things done within the bureaucracy. And because this is so at the level of the presidency, it is doubly so as Congress deals laterally with the bureaucracy at its various levels.

The President, at the apex of the executive hierarchy, will stand firmly in behalf of the bureaucracy only with respect to matters felt by him to be very important to his leadership and his program. On many matters he will appear rather neutral; beyond enumerating items in messages and budgets he can expend his time and energies on only a few things. On as many matters as possible he normally yields for the sake of his larger concerns.

The Congress thus through the President, and independently in working with the bureaucracy, exercises a great and wide influence on the executive branch. This general activity is augmented in particular formal procedures of hearing and comes to its peak in determinations with respect to organic enactments and decisions on particular appropriations. The appropriating power is an overriding sanction which causes congressional influence to penetrate to the remotest corners of the bureaucracy. Indeed, this is a power directly shared in by congressional secretaries and committee staffs; their influence sometimes is the most irresponsible in the national government, and sometimes is extremely able and responsible.

What is the total distribution of power over the bureaucracy, as between the President and the Congress, no one can say with assurance. It seems likely that the congressional power is many times the power of the President, with much of the congressional power exercised through individuals and committees rather than by Congress as a body. Yet the President as executive head of government has an important role even in this field of congressional interplay. His selection of ground on which to stand firm is important. And the fact that he can enlist his influence in any executive cause restrains Congress and its members at or near the boundaries of current practice. Those boundaries have principally but not clearly to do with interference, where members would determine without assuming responsibility for determinations.

Independent of his general prestige the President's resources in all this interchange are few. On rare occasions he may be able to allot a hospital or some other work to one area when on other grounds it would have been located elsewhere. But fifty congressmen may suspect that they are the losers and in common affront convert the President's political gain into a political loss. Then, too, the President will not wish, for its ill moral effects, often to require an agency to do something against its judgment of intrinsic operating values. Such use of incentives is actually extremely rare, much more often imaginary than real. Patronage, too, has almost vanished as a presidential resource. Very few of available appointments are of much consequence to members of Congress, and for each one who is pleased and helped by award of a job to a constituent, many others are offended. The value considerations in the selection of an appointee are usually too complicated to permit the appointments to be very useful in inducing congressional co-operation. A friendly word for a congressman's pet bill is more likely to have effect. Yet all such effects are short-lived; the general problem has much larger dimensions.

Actually the President's chief tangible resource is time for personal attention. News of conferences with the President is highly regarded as indicating strength and eminence to constituents. Physical limitations and other obligations limit the availability of time, however, so that even the basic communication with congressional leaders is perennially unsatisfactory. The rank and file usually feel almost wholly unrecognized.

The net of all this is to open the doors of our bureaucracy much wider than those of any other important state to the direct importunities of legislators and direct congressional determination of numerous particularities. This, then, constitutes a broad avenue of legislative control diverging in two directions: control in behalf of the general public as legislatively represented and control in many particulars in behalf of special constituencies, interests, and individual concerns. The net has a highly pluralistic content and an unintegrated character.

At the level of the President the moralities of this interchange have been largely suggested by its description. Nothing more venal can appear there than a change in allocation of works, which in functional terms is corruption of administration but which may be regarded in a second view as a subjective adjustment to the subtle political equities of which strictly administrative analyses would not take cognizance. Dealing with such equities is indeed intrinsic to the business of government, but it is business best done systematically, as in making budgetary allocations. The second view is therefore an unhappy one for those who take it, perhaps chiefly because it encourages more of the practice than even the practicalities seem to require. Such necessities are never so many as the weak and inexperienced may believe. The instance may be regarded as a species of compromise somewhere near the boundaries of present admitted practice, not without some similarities in lower levels of action. The cost may be viewed as an outlay of oil for creaking wheels of politics; if not defensible it is at least less in volume in the national government than the equivalent in commercial life. On the better side of the transaction there is a resemblance to many distinctly moral phenomena such as the expenditure of extra supervisors' time on a troublesome employee: that time is in the direction of good administration, but it, too, is at the taxpayers' expense. It is also to be remembered that notions of the medical fraternity which tend to dominate administrative plans for hospital locations, may not be as truly public-interest judgments as are more general and more political determinations.

Bureaucracy's Leader

The greatest ill effect of such actions is in the weakening of the administrative line. For all the executive government —and indeed for the political government as a whole—the obligation to support integrity is greatest on the President and on his staff, who partake of his influence. The obligation is greatest at that point because any deviation there multiplies itself in levels below. Lower levels are more vulnerable, and on them there is a moral obligation in behalf of responsible government to bend to presidential guidance. The President is actually in best position to take the highest moral ground, his obligation and dependence alike being pinned to the widest public.

No President, and indeed no public official, can take to his office the normal, private obligations of private friendship, or even the normal obligation and inclination to pay special heed to members of his family. For their advice and importunities, however honorable or valid, are irresponsible, outside of the context of the flow of systematic work responsibly delegated and reviewable. A special favor is no less a special favor when it is extended to a friend, and a special favor must be ever suspect when it is a bestowal made in the exercise of public responsibility. This moral restriction is one of many examples of the special exactions of public service, for it conflicts with practices normally rooted in the private morality of integrity in friendship and family relationships. Washington faced and recognized the problem soon after assuming office. He told a friend seeking an appointment: "You are welcome to my house; you are welcome to my heart. . . . My personal feelings have nothing to do with the present case. I am not George Washington, but President of the United States. As George Washington, I would do anything in my power for you. As President, I can do nothing."

Such chief-executive responsibility is generally most vulnerable at the level of the presidential personal staff, where responsibility is sometimes not easily or fully realized, where the dimensions of influence seem less than they do at the lower levels where the influence is felt, and where appreciation of the ways of systematic administration is sometimes lacking. President Franklin D. Roosevelt took great care to instruct his staff, and there is no known case of impropriety among those actually and personally responsible to him and selected by him; one exception was a vice-presidential protégé.

The administrative generalization is that at successively higher hierarchal levels direct intervention in the business of government should be successively less frequent and precise and the nature of control progressively more general. Difficulty is involved, however, in the words "more" and "less"; for a complete renunciation of the right to intervene, even very precisely, would be inimical to popular government as a renunciation of responsibility. There must be such a right, and if it is to be real it must be exercised occasionally. The occasional intervention will discipline and direct the whole administrative process, making it all subject to the influence of review; and this should be the primary, conscious, and systematic purpose of the intervention. The danger of corrupting administration then can be avoided if the interventions are themselves made systematically, with adequate staff work and with consideration preventive of whimsicality.

The administratively sophisticated understand these matters and avoid the painful efforts of the amateurs who feel that if only they can see the man at the top they can get what they seek. If it is a proper thing, they are much more likely to get it by prosecuting it at points, or in ways, in which it will reach the places where it may be systematically handled in context. The sophisticates thus avoid also the generally proper and effective resentments of lower-level executives when they see requests presented in terms of special influence. Mature and able members of Congress, for example, deal usually by preference with secretaries to high officials and by greater preference with lower-ranking officials.

The truth is that a citizen who rests his case on the exercise of special influence, unless he does it in ignorance, is usually, whether consciously or unconsciously, seeking special favor unavailable to those who cannot use that influence. The moral hackles of the bureaucracy rise in resistance, and it is central to the executive leadership of the President that he protect that morality.

It is also essential that the President have and exercise a centralizing control in response to public demand. It is only through the agency of the President and his systematic staff that the various functional specializations of executive government may be elevated from their preoccupations with special publics into a generally harmonious service of the whole public. This is the function of co-ordination and the function of leadership at the highest executive level. Appropriate and flexible organization and conduct of the staff of the executive office in the service of these functions is one of the most difficult and important of administrative problems. For the President as a person is first of all the chief figure in a presidential institution. It is only this which makes the job manageable in its unique significance. As an institution it is much more appropriate and feasible in our scene than any conception of "cabinet government." Of that we have no semblance, and for it no real capacity, some popular agitation to the contrary notwithstanding.

The executive office itself is still too little incorporated into public and departmental thinking. Even so sophisticated and able an administrator as General George C. Marshall never could bring himself to willing acceptance of such an institutional unit as the Bureau of the Budget. As Chief of Staff, Marshall was better equipped institutionally than the President, and of course he could not even have conceived of himself in his position not so equipped. Yet he somehow felt that the President must be limited to what he could do in his own person. Any such view would put the President at the complete mercy of the executive departments and would so reduce co-ordination as to leave the government a sprawling thing ill-equipped to serve the public and substantially less controllable by the public.

Realization of the dimensions of the presidential burden gives rise to many amateurish proposals directed toward lightening the burden. One such proposal is the perennial one of making the Vice-President a kind of "executive vice president." When he was Vice-President, General Charles Gates Dawes demonstrated unusually penetrating understanding by declining even to sit with the Cabinet. He wrote Calvin Coolidge that as a Vice-President he would have enough to do trying to support his chief in connection with deliberations of the Senate, but added, much more to the point, that the President should have as aides none with fixed terms and none not specifically named for the purpose by the President and readily removable by him.

A very similar proposal is for the establishment of a deputy, or assistant, president. The press on occasion has described one aide or another in that term. There never has been an official who actually so functioned, nor is there need for one. The conception of a deputy of general jurisdiction coextensive with that of the top officer is one that has no clear reality in any important and sustained practice. It may occur temporarily in an extraordinary association of two individuals. The peculiar responsibility of the President is generally inimical even to that rather fortuitous happening.

Essentially, the problem of the President, momentous as it is, is the rather familiar problem of adequate filling in of the graduated structure of the pyramidal hierarchy in which he inevitably stands at the apex. With a hierarchy so structured, the top position in any conceivable hierarchy is manageable in terms appropriate to it. Any hierarchy made necessary by social reality is as possible as the reality is real. The prevailing errors are two: seeing the presidential position in terms of more familiar and simpler hierarchal structures and attributing to familiar deputy titles a content beyond reality. Part of the essential underpinning of the presidency is in its institutionalized executive office. Another part is in the operating agencies. The latter is often wistfully simplified in terms of cabinet government.

Ministerial Responsibility

Actually there is rather less of cabinet government in parliamentary systems than most observers believe or than common terminology would suggest. Those governments are even more distinguished by something of greater significance for the United States, the deeply rooted practice of ministerial responsibility.

No President could do a halfway tolerable job by administering the executive branch through heads of departments and agencies alone, for the reason that the public interest cannot be sufficiently served by canceling out the pluses and minuses of the special interests inevitably represented by the departments and agencies. The public interest has much more content in many subtleties represented only through the totality of politics. That totality comes to bear on the executive branch adequately only at the point of the presidency.

The heads of departments and agencies do have, however, in bulk and substantive content the largest operating subordinate responsibilities. It is essential to the presidential responsibility that the pattern of control run to him through these important subordinates. This means for heads of departments and agencies the same capacity for control in their agencies as that described for the President in executive-governmental terms. Their posts also must be adequately staffed and institutionalized; authority auxiliary to their own must be subordinate and clearly susceptible to the kind of intervention already indicated as appropriate to the President but which must have that somewhat higher frequency suitable one level lower in the hierarchy. These objectives were generally advanced by the Hoover Commission recommendations, in recognition of the fact that the executive branch is too little controllable, too little responsible to the general public.

Further developments in this direction will bring us more ministerial responsibility, with the department heads, better subject to both President and Congress, contributing manageability to their higher responsibilities. It is the departmental or agency level at which public responsibility now begins to take on the character of the shell game Ross inveighed against.

It is only less true of department and agency heads than of Congress and President that they cannot in the first instance actually and narrowly be responsible for everything done. Similarly and more pointedly than in the case of Congress and President, the department and agency heads must be viewed as after the fact and in the last instance actually responsible for everything that has been done. For these officials are at the fringe of manageable public attention. If public responsibility was fixed below them, the public would have to guess continually under what shell the pea of responsibility might be located. And it is true that these officials can be made fully responsible and can be enabled to withdraw delegations and modify actions previously taken under delegations. It is true that through such review and intervention they may direct responsibly the course of day-to-day business. The number of bureau chiefs is much too large to provide an effective focus of general public attention; any focus on them could rarely be more than that of some special public, and this kind of limited concentration of attention will continue, and be more than ever appropriate, when the general public focus is fixed above them.

Following the provision of legal authority and the implementation of responsibility through structural arrangements and staff facilities, the reality of ministerial responsibility may be most advanced by the manner of congressional review. Assumption that heads of agencies actually are repositories of all responsibility for what is done in their agencies would raise the level of congressional performance to one more appropriate to the high congressional level. It would save Congress from playing the shell game, which is now the occasion for much of its own pettiness and frustration. It would more often raise in congressional minds the question whether a particular matter really merited secretarial attention. When anything does not merit attention of the secretary, it even less merits the attention of one's congressional colleagues. Such elevation in practice should in turn have consequences changing and improving the qualifications of men occupying the headships of departments and agencies.

The public should participate in the shift of perspective, of course. Congress is inappropriately overburdened by the flood of particularistic demands made upon its members by their constituents. The citizen somehow has tended to feel that his congressman would and should be able directly to determine the course of government in any and every particular, and members of Congress have not been skillful in educating their constituents and making their own loads manageable. Systematic individual and group setting of standards and treatment for constituent requests would make for a more responsible Congress. The more general public demands should flow to the President and Congress, the more particular to heads of agencies. The most particular demands should flow, as they tend to do, from small publics to the special bureaus especially dealing with them. Small publics are able to identify these more particular places of responsibility, and interchange at those lower levels is an inescapable and valuable factor of delicate differentiation in particular actions which serves the ends of pluralism. Such differentiations will be in fact better process if more clearly related to the higher scheme of integration.

The relationship between bureaus and special publics is implicit in programs affecting special publics. In these programs officials at lower levels are constantly exposed to members of the special publics and are thereby subject to a great deal of special-public control; such control is good insofar as it does not defeat general-public control.

There are other agencies, however, having relatively only general impact on the general public. The Department of State and the Department of Defense are vivid examples. For such agencies the concentration of ministerial responsibility tends to be more spontaneous so far as the public is concerned, but the method of Congress has not been proportionately differentiated. In the case of these two departments ministerial responsibility merges very quickly with presidential responsibility.

The development of ministerial responsibility will contribute to greater integration through more teamwork, but there is no tendency to excess in this direction. Rather, the pulls of diversity working through politics and government in this country will continue so pluralistic as generally to stretch unity exceedingly thin. In the present condition the Cabinet posts are peculiarly citadels of fragmentation, serving small publics very much more adequately than they serve the public.

The President himself will need to uphold ministerial responsibility in one rather crucial particular. This, as so often is the case in building and maintaining organizational responsibility, involves an ordinance of self-denial. Presidents too often tend to impose their own choices of undersecretaries, assistant secretaries, and deputies as heads of agencies. The practice undermines ministerial responsibility and contributes special difficulty to the problem of organizing for responsibility at the top agency level.

To many it may be a curious fact that there is in the government no definite pattern for the use of under- and assistant secretaries. They pose a problem somewhat akin to that of appropriate assignments for the Vice-President. The practice differs widely among agencies and within single agencies from time to time. The most common condition is that these officials of high title have little consistent power and very uncertain functions, though the general tendency is to use them more as the size and complexity of agencies increase. In the Justice and Post Office Departments the men of assistant-secretary rank are actually chiefs of bureaus. The problem of top-level organization will be one of enduring difficulty, but it will be clarified in one important connection as it becomes recognized that selection of under- and assistant secretaries is primarily the responsibility of heads of agencies, the President exercising only a right of approval and veto. These officials should also be removable by agency heads, with no more than nominal reference to the President.

The Taft-Hartley Act established in law one exceedingly troublesome violation of sound practice in the respect under discussion. It made the general counsel of the National Labor Relations Board independently responsible, a variation of bad practice complicated by a somewhat general inclination to elevate lawyers and legalistic procedure. The counsel became a storm center, and his independence was a serious impediment to the responsibility of the Board.

The chain of command is essential to responsibility. The necessity has successive applications at each level in the chain. Secretaries should appoint only the undersecretary, assistant secretaries, top members of their personal and departmental-institutional staffs, and bureau chiefs. Bureau chiefs should appoint only their assistant chiefs, their personal staffs, and heads of divisions; and so it should be on down the line, the upper levels in each case reserving approval and veto and determination of general selection practices. Subordinates cannot be held responsible unless they have discretion in their own houses. An important end for that exercise of discretion is achievement of the collegial effectiveness which is dependent on factors subjective and personal. The first essential to good personnel placement and to maintenance of responsibility which can be got at is that the person given an assignment be desired in that assignment by the official directly responsible for it.

The pattern of responsibility is intricate, important in its every part, and effective in terms of popular control only in all its parts together. Technical administration hereby, as in many other ways, is involved in the task of fundamental moral significance—achievement and maintenance of the reality of popular government.

While the basic, strictly administrative technique supporting responsibility may appear in most respects equally applicable to nonpopular government, it must be remembered that irresponsibility and democracy are not synonymous. Government in democracy must be unified in order to be responsibly democratic, as autocratic government must be unified in order to be autocratic.

The thing that distinguishes democracy is the character of the focuses of power, their popular nature and the popular nature of the forces working on them. These determine, not only in enactments of law and other formal products and procedures but also in countless and subtle overtones and undertones, essential moral elements, in some part produced in the course of public administration.

VII

ORGANIZATIONAL DANGERS

THESE pages deal largely with the use of public organizations and their systematic processes in pursuit of values. But not all aspects of organization are value supporting. Professor Robert K. Merton of Columbia University has brought together in *Social Theory and Social Structure* the more or less classical criticisms of bureaucracy regarded as complicated organization generally. These are primarily, although not exclusively, the criticisms formulated by sociologists, rather dominated by the Germanic, historically important but currently inadequate, views of Max Weber. As assembled they do not differentiate between governmental and other bureaucracies or between democratic and nondemocratic governmental bureaucracies. They do raise useful questions concerning values achieved or lost through the usual processes of organization. Rearranged, these criticisms are summarized in the following quotations:

1. The bulk of bureaucratic offices involve the expectation of life-long tenure. . . . Bureaucracy maximizes vocational security. . . . The bureaucrat's official life is planned for him in terms of a graded career, through the organizational devices of promotion by seniority.

2. The structure is one which approaches the complete elimination of personalized relationships and of non-rational considerations (hostility, anxiety, affectual involvements, etc.). . . . The impersonal treatment of affairs which is at times of great personal significance to the client gives rise to the charge of arrogance and haughtiness of the bureaucrat.

3. Bureaucracy is administration which almost completely avoids public discussion of its techniques, although there may occur public discussion of its politics. This . . . is held necessary in order to keep valuable information from economic competitors or from foreign and potentially hostile political groups.

4. Adherence to the rules, originally conceived as a means, becomes transformed into an end-in-itself. . . . They have a pride of craft which leads them to resist change . . . at least, those changes which are felt to be imposed by persons outside the inner circle of co-workers.

5. The transition to a study of the negative aspects of bureaucracy is afforded by the application of Veblen's concept of "trained incapacity," Dewey's notion of "occupational psychosis," or Warnotte's view of "professional deformation."

Merton explains admirably the three phrases quoted in the fifth criticism as follows:

Trained incapacity refers to that state of affairs in which one's abilities function as inadequacies or blind spots. Actions based upon training and skills which have been successfully applied in the past may result in inappropriate responses *under changed conditions*. An inadequate flexibility in the application of skills will, in a changing milieu, result in more or less serious maladjustments. Thus, to adopt a barnyard illustration used in this connection by Burke, chickens may be readily conditioned to interpret the sound of a bell as a signal for food. The same bell may now be used to summon the "trained chickens" to their doom as they are assembled to suffer decapitation. In general, one adopts measures in keeping with his past training and, under new conditions which are not recognized as *significantly* different, the very soundness of this training may lead to the adoption of the wrong procedures. Again, in Burke's almost echolalic phrase, "people may be unfitted by being fit in an unfit fitness"; their training may become an incapacity.

Dewey's concept of occupational psychosis rests upon much the same observations. As a result of their day to day routines, people develop special preferences, antipathies, discriminations and emphases. (The term psychosis is used by Dewey to denote a "pronounced character of the mind.") These psychoses develop through demands put upon the individual by the particular organization of his occupational role.

The concepts of both Veblen and Dewey refer to a fundamental ambivalence. Any action can be considered in terms of what it attains or what it fails to attain. "A way of seeing is also a way of not seeing—a focus upon object A involves a neglect of object B."

TENURE, EXPERTISE, AND CAPACITY

Systematic organization does generally put a premium upon tenure, and, being based on division of labor, it does pose the problems implicit in specialized ways of looking at things.

The pursuit of tenure is, to a degree, an administrative necessity, reflecting needs for continuity and the competence associated with familiarity. A new administration in any large organization would be ruined by any quick and wholesale turnover in personnel. The pursuit is also, to a degree, a result of the natural self-interest of incumbents. Their self-interest may easily exceed the requirements of good administration and may make for undesirable inflexibility, nonresponsiveness, and inertia. The pursuit is also partly a product of public opposition to favoritism, whimsicality, and the placing of political reward above public-service competence.

The pursuit of promotion by mere seniority is largely a product of the self-interests of incumbents politically reconciled among themselves into an excessive equalitarianism which tends to bring organizational performance to a dead level of mediocrity and to minimize incentive to excellence. Since all employees expect to increase in age, promotion by seniority is often uncritically accepted as "equal treatment." To some extent this expression of incumbent self-interest has public sympathy, and it may be the most common expression in this country of extreme equalitarianism, as it is certainly a reflection of a general concern for security.

Seniority does have some intrinsic claims and may be deferred to within narrow limits with gain and equity rather than at public or social cost. High turnover of personnel is extremely costly. Perhaps no new employee is as valuable on his job for a while as one who is an old hand at it. There is also a progressivism in the obligation of an organization to its employees which enlarges the obligation disproportionately as years of service increase. There is a common sense of an involved equity when an employee has given a large part of his life to a single organization, and often his services do have peculiar values. These values should not be confused, however, with hierarchal status, and it is the absence of adequate rewards for seniority as such which tends toward that confusion. In the national government in this country and in all civil service systems providing for "periodic promotions within grade," the tendency to promote hierarchally on a basis of mere seniority is lessened. In the national government the principal ill effects of concern for seniority inhere in a too rigid insistence upon promotion from within. Dynamism and responsiveness are served wherever there is systematic provision—and use—of means for some rather flexible recruitment at successive age and hierarchal levels.

The study of civil service practice throughout New York State by Dean Frank Piskor of Syracuse University indicates that the civil service movement has been retarded by efforts to install it too completely and too rigidly. Some of the leaders in national civil service movements readily admit that in some areas of government the civil service has been oversold, while in others it has been retarded by extravagant efforts in its behalf. Much of the civil service practice today —even much of so-called positive personnel administration— is actually opposed to opening the door to that responsiveness to the public which is the political good.

It is nevertheless to be remarked that in the national government civil service tenure has no such reality as is commonly attributed to it and that it is on the whole, in membership and placement of members, probably the most flexible civil service in the world. Its responsiveness also is unequaled elsewhere, but its responsiveness is overwhelmingly to small publics; it is in many ways lethargic with respect to the majority public.

Relative inattention to the large public is associated with functional specialization, which has two principal forms. In one form it is preoccupation with a single program which has incidence on, and is of concern to, a small public or several small publics which even when highly competitive together tend to constitute a larger, although still a minority, public. In its second form it is preoccupation with subject-matter *expertise*, as with economics, law, medicine, biology, physics, etc. Both forms lend themselves to "trained incapacity," "occupational psychosis," or "professional deformation"—and in government to political deformation. Professional public administration itself, of course, is not free from its own special tendencies of this sort. "A way of seeing is also a way of not seeing. . . ." Insofar as professional public administration assumes the special mission of subordinating administration to politics, it will minimize these tendencies. However, it will forever be in danger of becoming enmeshed in its own techniques.

Perhaps there is no single problem in public administration of moment equal to the reconciliation of the increasing dependence upon experts with an enduring democratic reality. It is a major problem in governmental morality in which center many subordinate value conflicts. The civil servant preoccupied with soil conservation has a moral conviction, and to an extent reflects a similar public conviction, that the whole future turns upon the conservation of this basic resource; he would tend to subordinate all other values to this.

The civil servant preoccupied with forest resources similarly would tend to subordinate other values to them. The military officer, charged with public responsibility for safeguarding national defense, not only puts that value first but is inclined to be impatient of other values and the processes by which they may be related and reconciled. The lawyer tends to look at the whole of government from the standpoint of his preoccupation. The economist is likely to feel that an "economic" decision not dictated by economists is inevitably immoral, forgetting that economics as a science offers little guidance to the moral. And so it goes, to specialization within specialization.

Merton, in another chapter of the book already cited, has struggled most unsuccessfully with the problem of the intellectual in bureaucracy, revealing a lack of understanding of organization and the way in which experts may serve organizations. It seems essential to recognize reality in a hierarchy of *expertise*, in which at successively higher levels experts become less expert and more generalist. Intellectuals happily are not all of one kind or order. Our problem often inheres in placing too high the too strictly expert, and very often in failing to recognize that when expert determinations are relied upon the reliance is a political delegation. Delegation to experts is always subject to political review and is made in the first place in a particular area according to the prestige of *expertise* in that area—"prestige" being a term reflecting political acceptability. Prestige in such matters is always limited by judgment of the importance of possible consequences regarded in nonexpert terms. The frustration of some experts is a reflection of an incapacity to impose the expert view; this is an unconscious authoritarianism in syndicalist form. In other cases expert frustration is a reflection of sheer unworldliness and particularly of an incapacity for complicated organizational performance.

Yet the social and public reality has been enormously enlarged in its technical content, and government must inevitably reflect and utilize this content. As a principal problem in public administration, this requires much learning both by administrators as such and by all experts who aspire to a participation in the management of affairs. In our government we have not distinguished enough, and not consciously enough, between the levels of *expertise*, and between experts and generalists. Nor have we put it deeply enough into our consciousness that the politician is the pre-eminent practicing generalist in democratic government. In the British civil service, top places are reserved much more consciously for the generally prepared and qualified.

The administrative task in its largest aspects, relevant to the role of experts, is to relate the functions and substantive contributions to each other and to the public service as a whole. More specifically, it is to organize against the limitations of trained incapacity, occupational psychosis, and professional and political deformation.

IMPERSONALITY

The criticism of bureaucracy as characterized by impersonality applies internally and externally, having values and dangers in both aspects. Internal impersonality involves a certain merging of members of the organization into an organizational entity, minimizing individual likes and dislikes and other personal concerns and maximizing an organizational rationale of order objectively concentrated upon organizational purposes. In highly complicated organizations with many parts devoted to special purposes, the most dramatic conflicts are between suborganizations, and the merging of individuals is primarily in the suborganizational group. There is, however, also an overriding merging into the larger organization. This grouping tends to several concentrations.

The supervisory unit has relatively slight significance, the section a little more, the division a little more, the bureau a great significance, the department a superior but less constant and less concentrated significance, and the government as a whole a still higher but more subtle and less concentrated sense of grouping. The phenomenon thus may be seen as not constantly in proportion to intimacy of association, but related to dependence on power and to coherence and importance in conception of mission.

The member actually loses less of individuality in these groupings than the observer is likely to believe; he finds the organizations, like all other human associations, serving as vehicles for the expression and development of his individuality. Yet impersonality is a substantial fact. It is impersonality chiefly with reference to work intrinsics, and this contributes to a maximization of the rational in a systematic performance highly free of whimsy. It is associated with a somewhat objective perception and weighing of distinctly personal abilities and attributes, and personality differences of course flavor the association here as elsewhere. Personalities require nice meshing, however, and organizational membership of this sort is inappropriate for those without a special temperamental affinity for it. The discipline of such associations may be mastered, and when mastered the discipline is capable of serving the ends of highly developed individualization. It is true, however, that the weak, the highly sensitive, the unskillful, and the extremely rugged individualist may be impersonally lost sight of or brushed aside—deprived of effective membership. Members who characteristically "make trouble" in these associations lose in influence and participation. Some of the trouble is legitimately to be regarded as a drag on performance, and subject to remedy only by the individual or by very special managerial attention. Some of it undoubtedly is an element of desirable dynamism sometimes beyond the capacity of the organization to incorporate. Good administration calls for special protection for these dynamic elements, as it calls for special managerial attention to more strictly individual personnel problems.

The impersonality associated with complicated organizational performance is generally valuable so far as the affected public is concerned. Its tendency is to systematize fair dealing and to avoid whimsy and discrimination—in other words, to provide a kind of administrative due process. The public can have general confidence that the treatment accorded one is the treatment accorded others. Impersonality does invite the charge of arrogance; the responsible official can rarely impress the citizen that he is listening intently to that citizen, because the official is at the same time under obligation to listen to those not present and to couch his response in terms of citizens generally. Niceties of language and manner in these communications have never been sufficiently studied or systematically used; they remain individual accomplishments and individual lacks. At best, however, the difficulty is considerable. Beyond manner and language there is also need to develop more sensitivity to, and responsible methods of, adjusting to nice differentiations in situations of individual citizens with respect to governmental programs.

To illustrate this point mention may be made of a problem once well resolved by the Farm Credit Administration. It was long recognized that dispossessed former owners of foreclosed farms often were superior prospects for purchase of those very farms; sentimental attachments made those farms more attractive to these men and their families and promised especially zealous efforts to meet future obligations. But because sales to these persons might appear to smack of favoritism, and in order to make a public record free from possibility of criticism, former owners were by rule excluded from purchasing their old farms, even when through relatives or friends they had secured ample down-payments. However, by setting up special review and certification procedures which would ensure against both the appearance and the reality of mere favoritism, sales to former owners were made permissible. Concern for human values of this sort and administrative ingenuity must combine to prevent certain ill effects of organizational impersonality and its public responsibility. High-level administrative leadership should recognize a special obligation to encourage regard for differentiating factors and in particular to encourage special flexibility and concern in behalf of the "little man" not possessed of resources or knowledge that would enable him to get attention available to the more privileged.

TECHNIQUES

The charge that bureaucracy is characterized by lack of public discussion of organizational techniques applies less to popular government than to almost any other bureaucratic form, but the very exception poses difficulty. The public is not generally familiar enough with the subject to discuss these techniques intelligently when attention is turned to them on the governmental scene. There is no general interdiction of such discussion. Indeed, there is a good deal of it, even though extremely amateurish and superficial. Beyond a certain point, perhaps, there is not much need for wide public discussion, but certainly organizational techniques should be open to such discussion insofar as the public has a sense of need for it, and some aspects of the subject do justify continuing public concern. These aspects have most to do with controllability. The public should insist on avoidance of independent status for governmental agencies, on avoidance of restrictions on chief executives' power to remove subordinate officials, and on the maintenance of clear, centralizing lines of responsibility. Given these things, the public can concentrate attention on the general public results of governmental programs and secure changes when unhappy about those results. Public interest in more technical aspects of administration may well await repeated and representative findings of critics in some degree specially qualified. Professional students of public administration may come in time to serve most helpfully in this way. It must be admitted, however, that up to now too few of them have penetrated enough of the reality deeply enough to serve. For the most part, too, the techniques they have learned most about are the techniques most remotely related to the subtler of democratic values. The techniques most studied have been those of "staff management," and generally at the point furthest removed from the conduct of programs, which are the end of public administration. There have been a few notable exceptions among students of the national government, but in general the greatest penetration in this respect has been in the more easily accessible and relatively simpler area of municipal government. One reason why popular fear of government is so concentrated upon the national government may be found in this fact that it is so little known, even to scholars.

The techniques that have been most studied are those of budgetary analysis and budget making, personnel administration including particularly classification, accounting, purchasing, organization methods, work measurements, workflow organization, and the like. In all of these considerable advancement has been made by extension of systematic staff performance in the last half-century, and great advancement has been made in the quality of some of the techniques. In these matters the national government compares rather well on the whole with other large organizations. Some of its lags, by professional standards, are attributable to congressional reluctance. Within the strictly administrative area a good many of the present shortcomings result from the normal expert tendency to elevate technique over purpose.

Such a tendency is somewhat implicit in separation of the so-called "staff" from the so-called "line"; there is a consequential lack of staff competence in, and exposure to, the programs of government. Prevalent theory about staff and line is unsatisfactory and misleading. It is commonly said by army officers, for example, in acceptance of the theory and in denial of their own knowledge that the army chief of staff is the line military commander in chief of the army, that the general staff is advisory, with no power of command. The usual practice in civilian, as well as in military, agencies is that staff offices do make determining decisions. When this is admitted recourse usually is had to the assertion, "But staff decisions are subject to appeal." Line decisions also are subject to appeal, and any such distinction can rest at most on relative frequencies of appeal. Actually, the distinction in frequency of appeal is slight if at all real, although insistence on the right of appeal from staff decisions probably contributes to the propriety of staff actions, as a similar insistence on the right of appeal in the line would contribute to the propriety of line decisions.

The reality of the relationship between line and staff is something extremely subtle, the product of long working together, and may be grasped fully only in experience. For systematic formulation, perhaps the best that can be hoped for is a series of different descriptions and an enunciation of different, even contradictory, theories. For the present purpose it may be helpful to suggest this as one description: that the line has to do with producing the program "product," and the staff has to do with general management of the whole operation, the two inevitably coming together at the top. When the staff becomes intoxicated with the technical projections of its specialization, a limiting guide would be provided by the question: "Is this something which the top man would really uphold as important to his general management of this organization?" Similarly, when the line becomes impatient over the "interference" of staff, a limiting guide would be provided by the question: "Would the top man agree with me that what I am resisting would more interfere with the turning out of product than it would advance his general managerial needs?" These two questions point to the strength and the weakness of both line and staff. And they point to a conflict of values, both of which have public importance. General management is the focus of general public responsibility. Program is the focus of differentiated public needs.

Accounting normally is done chiefly to satisfy the conventions of accounting. Its real purpose is to give to responsible administrators information helpful to them and through them helpful to stockholders or public. Accountants who know little of the needs of the administrators will do a job essentially technical. Where they are in a position of staff power, as particularly when they are headed by a comptroller, they will impose many practices of no particular value to the administrators and by the same token not contributing to good public reports. When budget examiners, at the bottom of the budget staff hierarchy, presume to "allow" or "disallow" estimates for particular personnel in a line operation for which they are not responsible, they are confusing a general managerial need to hold down expenses with a type of specific control that confuses and undermines responsibility. When classification specialists similarly use the rationalization of their technique to determine that an executive can or cannot have an assistant of a rank he feels necessary to his responsibility they are doing the same thing. Staff techniques need to point to generalized determinations recognizably important to general management, with particular determinations remaining at the point of program responsibility. Even more crucially, staff needs more willingly to defer to, and to implement, political determinations of policy. Often staff uses its techniques, in concern for technical values, to defeat the political policy. In the line the danger is somewhat similar: that in concern for special-interest values it will seek to defeat the general public purpose. Here, too, the failing is in a functional or technical preoccupation.

It must be recognized on the positive side, however, that staff offices constitute an organizational development especially dedicated to general-public responsibility and are in fact because of their integrating functions principal administrative citadels of majority government. While the operating programs of government are the crucial end product of public administration, they serve the public best, not as sprawling, unco-ordinated, and autonomous differentiations of governmental effort, but as operating differentiations under systematic pulls toward integration. The interaction of line and staff therefore has a vast deal to do with maximizing differentiated values by rationalizing those values with respect to the values of majority government. Staffs at every principal level of executive governmental responsibility in this country tend to be undermanned and inadequately led. Because they have intragovernmental functions, properly involving little direct dealing with the public, they are insufficiently appreciated.

DYNAMICS VERSUS RIGIDITY

Much of what has been said in the foregoing discussion bears upon the criticism that bureaucracy tends to be inflexible and unyielding. In its most important special aspect this criticism was expressed by Dewey as a lack of recognition of newly emerging publics. While organization conducted without imagination and under little political pressure does have rigidity and a tendency to exclude the dynamic, there are ways particularly to organize for the better achievement of flexibility and dynamism. In simplest terms this involves fixing special responsibility for these values hard to achieve and supporting that responsibility with resources. In addition administrative leadership has an obligation to discourage the tendency to timidity and to create an atmosphere hospitable to flexibility, imagination, better processes, and a penetrating concern for citizens as individuals.

In general, however, it must be said that the traditional criticisms of bureaucracy presented at the beginning of this chapter ignore the effects of politics and therefore apply very much less to the American government than to most other bureaucracies. Under political control and penetrated by the concern for acceptance dictated by that control, the basic source of governmental flexibility, dynamics, and considerateness is the public. The immediate vehicle of the public is politics, which in the United States travels more roads than in any other nation. Criticisms set forth here are counsels of improvement. Even now the net of the American governmental performance is far less alarming than it is reassuring. Far from involving regimentation in police-power terms, rough and arbitrary, it is shot through with persuasion, cooperation, inducement, service, and considerateness. As the domestic government has grown, it has moved out among the people, working with them, seeking their favor, subjecting itself to their influence.

What danger there is lies chiefly in another direction; that the power of the government may be too slight in support of the majority public. The very skill of the bureaus in getting support of small publics raises barriers to the achievement of majority positions. The charge that the government regiments, and the charge that bureaus build power blocs, in canceling each other raise this other question: Is our complex totality too confusing because of the frustration of a too-inchoate majority?

VIII

PRESSURE GROUPS

Public administrators, says Leonard White, "stand in the midst of scores of conflicting, competing, cooperating, overlapping groups whose efforts to 'guide' administrators are never ending." Going on from there, Pendleton Herring in *Public Administration and the Public Interest* has written that Congress to an increasing extent has escaped the onus of directly settling group conflicts, placing upon the shoulders of the bureaucrat "the burden of reconciling group differences and making effective and workable the economic and social compromises arrived at through the legislative process." Going further, he has pointed out that officials "in building 'public' support for their agency sometimes create a political machine of their own; the bureau builds a place for itself in the community and makes demands on Congress in the name of the 'public welfare.'" Going very much further he has proposed a thesis: that "the greater the degree of technical control the government seeks to exert over industrial and commercial groups, the greater must be their degree of consent and participation in the very process of regulation, if regulation is to be effective or successful."

Carrying this logic still further in the *Public Administration Review*, Norton Long has militantly upheld agency efforts to build power bases, on the ground that without such efforts our government provides no focus of power sufficient to the needs. Speaking from a background of experience in the Office of Price Administration, he reflected particular concern for power to carry through an activity reflective of little conscious self-interest other than the truly public self-interest in successful conduct of war. Herring's proposed thesis related to a continuing activity of government originating also in a public concern which he would dilute to the extent necessary for effectiveness.

REPRESENTATIVE BUREAUCRACY

These various references emphasize the essentially political nature of public administration and identify the ubiquitous and varying problem commonly associated with interest or pressure groups. They impute a certain representative character to the bureaucracy which Charles Wiltse has described as pertaining to special interests and has attributed to a need not adequately met by the geographical representativeness of the legislature:

It is only with the rapid spread of industrialism coincident with and subsequent to the Civil War that representation in Congress ceased to be in effect functional. The railroad and the telegraph served to break down sectional barriers, and economic and cultural interests thereafter cut too sharply across state lines to be adequately represented on a geographical basis. At the same time, the impact of technology forced Congress to deal with the highly complex problems of a rapidly changing economic and social structure. The law-making machinery was unequal to the task, the trained expert was introduced, and executive and legislative functions tended to merge. Thus the purposes of functional representation came to be accomplished through the creation of administrative agencies.

There is surely considerable validity in this view, but it is also true that the bureaucracy has in addition to the representation of particular interests other functions which call for representativeness in a different sense and for administrative performance reflective of additional responsibilities.

A truly representative bureaucracy is in its several parts

variously representative of special functions and interests, and highly representative altogether of the public at large. Government cannot properly be merely a reflection of private interests. Its machinery must provide for recognition of, and deference to, private interests while reconciling, translating, and sublimating these interests into something resembling the public interest.

Reasonably complete representativeness therefore calls for flexibility in personnel recruitment and assignment, personnel widely drawn, personnel and organizational units representative of diverse functional capacities, and organizations structured and managed to effect co-ordination oriented to public control. This view is distinctly hostile to such practices as that of the Forest Service, which limits recruitment to graduates of forestry schools.

Here as elsewhere in the present discussion "public control" is viewed as a capacity for public control, not as its universal or constant exercise. Even so, the discrimination thus implied calls for governmental and public sense and character, not functional sense and character alone.

Flexibility in recruitment and assignment of personnel qualifies tenure in general and rights of employees assumed to attach to particular job assignments. The need for this flexibility is greatest in the immediate offices of the President and heads of departments and agencies, in the top two levels of their staff units, in the level of bureau chiefs, in staffs of bureau chiefs, and occasionally among division heads within bureaus. The degree of flexibility required diminishes somewhat at the lower of the points listed, there involving less actual job mortality and more of mere changes in assignment. Ordinary turnover figures have little significance with respect to this kind of flexibility, since the figures reflect chiefly changes in the lower grades, and there have been no systematic and comprehensive studies of the reality of change in the levels here under discussion. Prevailing practice gives much greater flexibility than is commonly recognized, but usually does not approach the limits possible and desirable under sophisticated direction.

The development of power by bureaus, mentioned in the introductory quotations, is probably proper and useful up to a point, not only in the absence of a sufficient use of parties but intrinsically as implicit in the performance of the interest-representation function. With existing dimensions of pressure groups the development of parties as more often determinants of majority positions and improved administrative practices might be looked to for sufficiently limiting bureau power at that point beyond which it would be injurious.

Under present conditions the ordinary bureau may be regarded as merely contributing useful grist to the political mill, or—in a more appropriate form of the figure—as usefully operating certain bits of the political mill's machinery, posing no concentration of political power not readily enough subordinated to the power system. As pressure groups and their governmental representative agencies become more and more consolidated in the form of a few very large and disproportionately effective minority power blocs, even very greatly strengthened parties and their publics would be placed at a serious disadvantage. In those conditions many human values prized by members of the great interest groups as well as by others, and not at all represented by the consolidated groups, would be lost in the shuffle. This would constitute monopoly in a new dimension, more evil than any up to now faced or contemplated. It would reverse the role of private interests as champions of pluralism, converting it into the role of machines of political regimentation.

This thought qualifies conventional notions about executive organization in terms of "coherent missions," pointing toward a somewhat incoherent structure for particular agencies, so that they may be preliminarily representative of functional concerns approaching public character. In the private scene highly varied and competitive interest groups susceptible to balance-of-power management are essential, not only to a corresponding pluralism, but also to the greater pluralism involving values not represented by consolidated pressure groups. Such values now find political ingress through interstices of varied interest demands. They provide priceless elements in the area of discretion available to leadership.

It is in the need to defer to special interests, the accompanying need to reconcile special interests, and the overriding need and capacity for injection of the public interests, that administrators—like others politically responsible—face their most demanding moral dilemmas.

Herring's tentatively offered thesis might appear to justify an almost total abandonment of public responsibility. He intended no such implication, of course, although it is often charged that regulatory agencies do become mere creatures of the interests regulated. What Herring intended to convey is the need to temper compulsion and to fix it at the point where—in view of the public temper as well as the private-interest temper—it will be accepted, effective, and successful. Obviously, in different agencies at different times and in different situations there are wide variations in strength and skill. Regulatory agencies, isolated and therefore not structured for co-ordination with other than their special interests and otherwise confined in procedural ritual and removed from direct impact of the wide public forces, do tend to fix the point of compulsion at a point only slightly ahead of free acceptance by those regulated. Strong leadership in any such agency is held near the common denominator determined by weak precedents.

Where the transactions regulated or otherwise affected are the clear and special concern of competing private interests and the governmental function is first of all to find the point of balance between the two (or more) forces, there is a somewhat automatic movement of decision some distance in the direction of the public interest. Sometimes the result is a rough approximation of the public interest; this is true when the public is substantially satisfied when the conflicting interests are satisfied and in balance. In these cases, too, governmental compulsion is not heavily felt or considered notably arbitrary, since those who are in conflict recognize the strength of identified private opponents and defer to the need for compromise.

There are intermediate areas in which a partial and preliminary resolution of the problem, by compromising conflicting interests, contributes to a movement toward other determinations of sufficiently public-interest character. For example, when various chambers of commerce and other interests propose a number of reclamation projects and existing projects resist the proposals out of competitive fears, private agreements worked out through such an agency as the Reclamation Association will tend to approach the reclamation-public interest, and the general public interest will be sufficiently served first by general determinations affecting the allocation of public funds to the reclamation function and second by general administrative guidance and co-ordination. But here, as in all conflicts of interest, there is a need for constant reference to, and strengthening of, the larger public interest. Therein is the problem of how much "compulsion" to use. In many cases the problem is how much influence and suasion and ingenuity to use short of what might be felt as compulsion.

The reconciliation of interests reaches dimensions of greatest administrative difficulty when the conflict is between a strong private interest or interests and a public interest real but unorganized and effectively mute. The consumer interest typifies such a public interest. All persons have the concern of consumers, but it is a concern not organized or effectively channeled, so that its influence is immeasurably less than its intrinsic dimensions. The highly organized producer interest is overwhelmingly dominant, therefore, and the consumer interest is rationalized into an income interest believed to be comprehended adequately in the producer interest. The income interest in turn divides into concerns for business income, labor income, farm income, and general distribution of income. The income interest lends itself to organization much better than the consumer interest.

Various other strong public interests find organization difficult. The housing interest in recent years, for example, has been intrinsically much stronger than it has been effective. An interest so strong and particular may be given organization by exercise of public leadership. The great interest in employment was given organization by Senator James E. Murray of Montana; his Full Employment Bill, once introduced, struck so popular a note that it was quickly passed, long before its proposals had attained any substantial feasibility. The administratively devised Stamp Plan was channeled to effective public support by administrative organization of various private-interest relationships. But generally there are very real public interests not readily brought into contrast with acute and strong private interests, and almost throughout the area of public administration officials must struggle with the problem of how much, how far, and in what way to insist upon these public interests. The inner moral satisfaction of responsible administrators turns on the degree to which they have been able to inject consideration of the public interest in the face of a natural inclination of spokesmen for private interests to see those interests as the undiluted public interest.

Neither the simple reconciliation of private interests nor their reconciliation modified by considerations of public interest is in the end a technical performance, no matter how many technical factors may figure in it. It is a political function, involving essentially the weighing of forces and the subjective identification of the narrow area within which these forces may be balanced and the exercising of discretion concerning the point within that area at which acceptability and public interest may be effectively and properly maximized. One of the most dramatic examples of the function is in labor-management mediation of nationwide differences when they develop in some essential industry. Public policy and public interest at the present time point first to giving play to collective bargaining; as public damage becomes substantial and threatening, public interest turns quickly to public mediation; as the damage and threat increase, the public interest turns sharply to settlement, with less and less concern for the positions of those involved in the controversy. At the later stage, governmental action is possible—and necessary—which would not have been acceptable at an earlier stage. Administrative appraisal of the successive stages is of the essence of the function.

ADMINISTRATIVE TECHNIQUES

Usually in less dramatic ways, with smaller forces engaged, these same elements penetrate a large part of the whole area of public administration. The kind of skill required has not been as consciously sought and developed as it should have been, yet under the pounding of time and necessity great skill of the appropriate sort has come to characterize government. Weakness is on the side of deferring to the special interest.

In the process of administration this problem of balancing private and public interests takes many particular forms. At the coming into office of a new Cabinet member, the representative of one interest introduced himself to the new aides of the new department head by explaining that he had been in the habit of walking to the office two or three times a week with the preceding secretary, and expressing the hope that he would have the same friendly relationship with the new one. Another interest quickly shifted Washington representatives in order to send there a college classmate of the new secretary. Still another elevated a friend of the new secretary to the presidency of their organization, and a number of others retained as their attorney a close personal friend of the secretary. Each of these moves had to be met with appropriate administrative protections. One improvised rule was that no interest representative of that particular kind could have an appointment to see the secretary except in the presence of the solicitor of the department. The rule was not feasible in the case of the attorney, who was invariably a house guest of the secretary when he came to Washington; in that case a clear understanding was reached with the attorney, who was a meticulously honorable man. Agencies in the department were alerted to the particular need of avoiding any appearance of favoritism in all these cases, and the net result for the interests was a firmer stand with respect to them than might otherwise have developed.

Another device of interest representatives is to identify the offices where a particular bit of business is in its initial stages and then to prosecute their requests at every one of the dozens of offices to which it subsequently moves. Such a practice goes far beyond the bounds of due consideration, seriously impedes the handling of work, and requires preventive administrative measures. Particular facilities need to be established for the consideration of interest proposals, simpli-

fying the process for the interest groups and for administrators alike.

Agriculture groups in the Department of Agriculture,
labor groups in the Department of Labor and kindred agencies, business groups in the Department of Commerce and
the Reconstruction Finance Corporation, railway representatives in the Interstate Commerce Commission, and others
similarly in other agencies inevitably have a special access,
and this requires administrative weighing along with other
factors.

It is to be understood that to a certain extent and in many
particulars all the interest groups wish is attention which
reassures as to forthcoming fairness. They all have some
sophisticated recognition of points beyond which their interests cannot be served and at least some inclination to defer
to official responsibility. In a certain degree little more is
expected than to be able to report to their own organizations
visits with appropriate officials, though these expectations as
a whole far exceed the physical capacity of those officials
the interest groups regard as appropriate. In other instances
a small action of concession is highly prized as demonstrating
effectiveness and influence. In still other cases extremely
laborious negotiation is called for.

Though much of all this business may be and is initiated
through "the Secretary's Office," only an extremely small
part of it can be conducted there, and of course a much
smaller part with the secretary individually. In general the
more extensive the consultation and negotiation, the lower
the administrative level at which it must take place. A very
great deal of it begins and ends at one very minor office, very
much of this in "the field" rather than in Washington. Next
in amount is that volume which involves some kind of appeal
at one higher office, and so on up to the residuum that reaches
the very top. This is a normal process of administrative ap-

peal, sometimes carried very far in highly unwarranted fear, sometimes carried equally far in righteous indignation, and sometimes carried similarly in pride or highly determined self-seeking.

The extent to which this process of appeal is carried is a rough index of unhappiness, and a rougher index of strength as related to unhappiness. Intensity of feeling on the part of affected citizens is always, and strength of those citizens is usually, important in the administrative weighing of the business; indeed these are principal measures of importance along with administrative judgment of general public importance. According to these measures, therefore, importance is reflected in the level at which administrative attention more serious than facilitation and courtesy is completed. This completion is associated with an assumption of responsibility at that level, and very often with specific delegation of responsibility to that level. Specific delegations of this kind are made in the course of administrative consultation concerning the particular matters at the levels at which the delegations are made. Lack of confidence that a decision will stand up under later complaint is always the occasion for upward reference. The administrative process is in high degree this business of handling trouble or the possibility of trouble by a process of reference between levels.

Administrative appeal is resorted to after the fact as well as before, of course, and this appeal is often a test of the adequacy of the previous procedure and the propriety of earlier assumption of authority at a particular level. The possibility of appeal after the fact shapes action before the fact to the closest possible approximation of a decision that will withstand later review. After-the-fact appeal is always handled at a series of levels ranging at least one level higher —usually two—than the before-the-fact appeal. The possibilities end only with Congress, or in some particulars with the courts. Repetition of appeal similarly as an index of intensity of feeling pushes review steadily higher in the hierarchy.

Effectiveness of appeal is by no means directly proportional to the private power involved. Appeals from single citizens are generally pushed hierarchically upward in exactly the same fashion, and in many cases where nice human values seem to be involved, they get disproportionately extended attention.

In all such matters the secretary and his office can and do determine important shadings in policy attitudes in a wide variety of ways. Letters addressed to the secretary are all read, some by as many as a half-dozen different members of different ranks, in the secretary's office, and there referred for handling in widely varying ways. A first letter from a single citizen or some fairly large interest group may be referred to the bureau concerned "for direct reply." A second appeal may be referred to the bureau for "preparation of reply, signature Assistant to the Secretary." A third appeal may be sent to the bureau for "preparation of reply, signature Under Secretary," a fourth might call for "signature Secretary," a fifth might call for a memorandum of report critically reviewing the whole matter, and a sixth might result in a special investigation. Conversely, after the third appeal all letters might be referred to the bureau for direct action. Each of the earlier steps indicated would reflect a growing concern in the secretary's office, leading to more and more stringent and higher reconsideration in the bureau. The shift to direct and final reference to the bureau, on the other hand, would indicate secretarial satisfaction in the original determination. Many procedural variations of similar sort have a pervasive effect on departmental actions.

In general this process of appeal is a process of review in terms of successively broader responsibilities and diminished technical concern. The rigidities of some fixed procedure which down the line appear essential to administrative order or technical conformity, up the line appear less important than citizen unhappiness and essential equity. Similarly, the special interest preoccupying a lower level is weighed at the higher level in relationship to many special interests and a more general interest, for these are the differences in responsibility that are the occasion for the hierarchal structure. Hierarchy thus provides in a systematic but subtly varying procedure values commonly thought to be had only through boards. In most matters the chief virtue of a board is not administrative but political; this virtue is in its seeming assurance of a group judgment, which is the invariable necessity in hierarchal performance. Indeed boards would be largely futile without supporting hierarchies. In some matters, as when it is necessary to give high public assurance of nonpartisanship, boards have a real usefulness, although less than is commonly believed.

Use of hierarchy as here outlined is of the very essence of bureaucratic performance, and this essence is reflective of the values attainable through organized effort, the reality of which should not be obscured by criticisms of bureaucracy. The essence is first of all a constant development of, and reliance upon, group judgments at each of successive hierarchal levels, these levels providing judgments in terms of differentiated exposures and responsibilities.

The first administrative technique protective of moral values, therefore, is in a lateral sharing of judgment and responsibility, using not only the whole capacity represented by the group but also the strength, resistance, and resiliency of the group. The second technique is the invocation of responsibility at the next and successively higher levels. Those whose combined strength seems inadequate for injecting into any bit of business as much public-interest value as seems to them imperative have the recourse of reference upward and reliance upon the greater strength represented by the higher level.

Some other special intraorganizational structural and procedural arrangements are essential to good handling of private-interest concerns. For example, it is probably generally desirable for the solicitor's office to have department-wide scope and for all attorneys employed as attorneys to be members of the solicitor's staff rather than to serve as bureau attorneys. There may be some exceptions in the cases of very large bureaus where intrabureau arrangements of comparable sort may be achieved; the Bureau of Internal Revenue is probably such an exception. But in every case it appears desirable to have a departmental solicitor with staff sufficient to serve as a superior, reviewing legal office, where review of procedure will be given in terms clearly secretarial. Similarly, all other departmental staff offices should be recognized as playing important parts in the process of administrative review, their terms of reference being solely secretarial. In the Department of Agriculture, for many years the Office of Budget and Finance under William A. Jump was of crucial importance to the function of review in public-interest terms. All secretarial staff offices represent a very great enlargement in the secretary's capacity to review, direct, and integrate his department. A large and varied department so equipped brings its business into broader, more public focus with much greater ease than smaller and more simply homogeneous departments or agencies.

The creation of the solicitor's office as a secretarial staff establishment apart from the bureaus is mentioned particularly as one item contributing to the separation of functions resembling prosecution and adjudication. Substantial separation of such functions is normally a hierarchal necessity, particularly in large organizations, but some special structural arrangements are wholly in order, not only to ensure the separation but to make it plain to a critical public. Most government business does not closely resemble prosecution and adjudication, but some of it does; and values not wholly unrelated are involved, if subtly and variously, in other business. Division of assignments as between units of a bureau, as between bureaus, and as between bureaus and staff offices may be particularly and consciously utilized to serve values often felt to be protected only by the courts. One of the primary functions of structure and procedure alike is to determine levels at which decisions of various kinds may be responsibly made, and to enforce cross reference and coordination as means to the end of balanced judgment.

It is to be remembered that many interest groups are concerned with a particular governmental agency only rarely, and that too definite procedural arrangements for them would be unnecessarily cumbersome. There are values, too, in a somewhat free-and-easy coming and going of these expressions and absences of expression and concern. The totality of the whole interest-group reality is served by such flexibility, and this service in turn opens the way to more interests altogether than would a too formal and rigid provision for it. This open door to multiple interest groups contributes a more truly public character to the performance than would a more restricted and definite provision that would amount to special privilege.

It is even more to be remembered, however, that almost never does a pressure group whose interest is simply the public interest descend upon a Washington department. Sometimes such groups do visit the White House and Capitol. The preponderance, however, is wholly with the special interests, and at the departments and agencies the concerns of those who come and those who write are almost exclusively special interests. These are, of course, by no means to be disregarded. But they put the public interest very much at a disadvantage and pose for administrators their chief problems in value conflicts.

Another disadvantage faced by the public interest is in the difficulty of organizing, and the present generally inadequate organization of, facilities for carrying public-interest consideration systematically to the *interdepartmental* level. The only substantial facilities for this are three: certain coordinating offices for particular relationships between a few agencies having special need of interchange; interdepartmental committees; and the staff offices of the President, including the President personally. The staff offices do not have scope equal to the problem, interdepartmental committees are cumbersome and often cannot be given responsibility equal to the difficulty, and the co-ordinating departmental offices reflect only spotty efforts of varying degrees of adequacy in a limited number of areas.

Toward Better Performance

The results as a whole are rather better than these lacks suggest, simply because of a penetrating effect of diverse political sentiments and forces. The basic safeguard is, as has been emphasized repeatedly in these pages, where Woodrow Wilson pointed long ago when he said: "To fear the creation of a domineering, illiberal officialism is to miss altogether the principle upon which I wish to insist. That principle is, that administration in the United States must be at all points sensitive to public opinion." To make this abidingly and increasingly true is in one part the great task of administrators. It will be done generally in ways similar to those suggested here, and not through sentimental efforts to incorporate small numbers of private citizens into the administrative process through advisory committees or the delegation of governmental authorities to citizens not governmentally responsible. Such limited and special citizen participation cannot be actually so representative of the *public* as is the government and cannot be responsible as is the government. Citizen desires for participation may more appropriately be directed toward political activity.

Nothing is so representative of the public as the product of the totality of our political processes. Nothing is so good a governmental tool for the public as the government itself. Reforms needed to improve this tool in its capacity to serve more the general interest are political and intragovernmental reforms.

One needed intragovernmental reform has to do with restricting the movement of government officials to employment as lobbyists by interest groups. There is now rather satisfactory practice, supported by some specific laws, administrative regulations, and general administrative scrutiny, with regard to gainful personal activities on the part of employees in fields at all associated with their official activities. This practice can be considerably improved, but the general record is admirable at the national level. More concern is warranted about the influence on those never actually hired away exercised by the possibility that they might be.

The number of officials who do move into such employment is trivial in relation to the whole official body. Those who are hired for lobbying in the executive branch are also, in fact, bad bargains for the lobbies; the agencies in self-protection erect extraordinary barriers to the lobbying effectiveness of former associates. The corrupting influence is exercised before their employment, and it is an influence on a larger number than those who are actually hired by the interest groups. Any effective action in prevention of this element in public administration is open to some criticism as an impairment of what may be regarded as normal personal rights. It would probably involve, for example, public and rigid exclusion from executive offices and association of all former officials so employed for the period of their expected special usefulness to the lobbies. Some such penalties may well be regarded, however, as a proper corollary to public service.

But the most constant problem is one that confronts every official and every agency in a large percentage of the actions they take. It is faced in the question pointing to the manner and degree in which the interests of single citizens and citizen groups are to be reconciled with the general public interest: "How much and in what way shall I insist upon the injection into this matter of strictly public considerations?" Better answers to this question depend in the end upon individual administrators, their understanding, their attitudes, and their effectiveness.

No single government program expresses the complete interest of any citizen. Perhaps no single government program expresses an interest recognized by every citizen. Some government programs strain the limits of enlightened self-interest of many citizens, who regard those programs as beneficial to others but not beneficial—perhaps even injurious—to themselves. Good public administration in concern for acceptability and other democratic values must take account of such differences in citizen attitudes.

This is true even when a program is distinctly a majority program and even when its only occasion is a strictly public need generally recognized—as in the conduct of war. In managing the war program the administrator must be concerned to go beyond his special responsibility and preoccupation in order to defer as much as possible to parents of those in military service, the necessities of civilian supply, protection of civil liberties, and many other interests and values. The extent of the deference required will vary according to the development of popular expectations, and the popular recognition of the urgencies of the battlefront. Spontaneous administrative deference will vary according to administrative judgment of the same urgencies. The appropriate administrative decision will fall somewhere between these two, and the problem is in identifying "somewhere." Here sound decision making dilutes a clear and urgent public interest with factors deriving from other public interests and from private interests.

In all program fields the problem is basically the same, varying widely in content according to variations in size and nature of publics affected. Where the program is a high-priority majority program—a relative rarity outside of war and prosecution of gross crime—the moral administrative effort should be to seek flexible dilutions of the majority insistence with a factor of empathy for minorities and individuals. Much more commonly, a program has clear and strong majority character, but the particular majority effectively forms only on dramatic occasions, whereas in contrast the minority especially impinged upon is large and disproportionately effective. In such situations the moral responsibility is to push persistently in support of the somewhat inchoate majority. Very commonly a program has only majority assent, benefits of the program accruing chiefly to some special public. In this case the responsibility of the administrator will vary according to the effectiveness of the beneficiary public. His obligation will be generally to temper the program with considerations of other public interests. The larger the dimensions of the program and the more powerful the beneficiary public, the heavier this obligation should rest on him. The weaker and less privileged the clientele, the greater should be the administrator's concern to realize the full dimensions of the majority assent.

These are counsels offsetting the tendencies of weakness and pedestrianism, pointing generally toward fulfillment of majority government tempered by a penetrating concern for minorities and individuals. They are related to the present administrative reality, a complete picture of which would reveal a vast reflection of our society's pluralism, the very antithesis of a concentration of regimenting power. It is a picture too confusing to the public as a public, on the whole insufficiently useful as a tool of the public, and more useful to special publics.

In nearly all administrative decisions the sense of virtuous performance is to be pursued by attempting to inject some increased allowance for the more public interest and some increased concern for those citizens not immediately present or heard. In this pursuit there must be care not to confuse one's professional viewpoint, functional preoccupation, or personal prejudices with the public interest. There must also be willingness to take without frustration or cynicism that public-interest gain found to be feasible, and with buoyancy to remain on guard and to continue the effort on later occasions.

Private citizens may help, by trying more often to think of themselves as members of the public. The public's advocates are far too few, their strength much too weak, their efforts much too spasmodic. Citizens need to support, as politicians and administrators need to devise, ways in which protections, incentives, and rewards stimulate and reinforce administrative pursuit of the public interest, counterbalancing the private-interest forces which propel along the path of weakness.

IX

ADMINISTRATIVE LOYALTY

CONSIDERATION of the executive handling of pressure groups has pointed up the constructive importance of organizational performance. Pressure groups cannot be well or sufficiently handled by any single official, high or low; good administration in this as in other respects results from an intermingling of value judgments and responsibilities. The intermingling required brings into focus the values of some officials intimately but variously associated and acquainted with the relevant special interest and the values of other officials more widely exposed and more widely responsible. The processes of a public executive organization viewed altogether thus have great bearing upon the moral achievements and failings of government. The personal traits, values, and functions of individual officials have an equally obvious bearing, and require equal consideration. The organization and the individual interact and are mutually dependent upon each other. The problems of morality press hard and often upon individual public administrators. Even so, they are distinguished by their organizational context.

The context, indeed, is multiple organizational. Public officials in the United States not only deal with this reality, they are of it and reflect it in their own individualities. They are members of families, and family obligations inevitably color their judgments and qualify their daring. Many other associations branch out from the family, all contributing factors of discipline and loyalty. Identification with a profession is a personal matter also involving organizational values diverging from those attaching to the particular job. So far as his working situation is concerned, an official's individual values are, first of all, composites derived from other associations. In his job, too, his responsibilities point no single way. He has responsibilities to his immediate superiors, colleagues, subordinates, to his section, division, bureau, agency, to the President, to the Congress, to "the government," to particular publics, and to *the* public.

The intermingling of personal moralities—already in individual terms highly complicated—and the adjustment of that intermingling with official organizational moralities is an important aspect of public administration. This organized intermingling and adjustment involve a discipline, and the key word in this discipline is "loyalty." The problems of morality are not solved for the individual official, however, by knowing the key word. The problems are in conflicting or divergent loyalties. Integrity appears not often as an integer. One loyalty often will require some related disloyalty. Even though in a particular case the individual may decide that one loyalty takes precedence over another, the decision is stressful, and in many such decisions there can be no clear, agreed-to hierarchy of loyalties. Organizational performance can, and does, involve some substitution of organizational hierarchy of responsibility for a sheer philosophical, or a completely individual, hierarchy of moralities. Organizational sense involves in part an ability to be moral and to have a sense of being moral while contributing one's value judgments to organizational performance and at the same time relying upon the responsibility of the hierarchy. It involves some kind of treaty between one's individual responsibility and the responsibility of others. This means at once pushing for the good as one sees it and not taking one's self too seriously. But the treaty must be often renegotiated.

Without it an official may lose the better in striving for the unattainable best, or at the other extreme may hold stubbornly to a good so specific and narrow that it actually excludes many other goods.

The moralities of loyalty do have some hierarchal structure. One may be loyal to family and to state at the same time, may indeed recognize the two loyalties as being complementary and as being only two in a long chain of intermediate loyalties similarly complementary. One may be loyal to state and at the same time be loyal to humanity in general. But one may not be loyal to, or maintain full membership in, two different families in identical functional terms, for this impairs the hierarchy of relationships. Nor may one be loyal to one state and more loyal to another state not organically related in terms involving different functions. These things reflect hierarchal relationships common in the experience of men, generally understood even if unformulated verbally. Anything much resembling treason, to which temptation is slight, is therefore a rarity anywhere, never to be expected to appear with much frequency apart from a general societal illness and disintegration not hard to recognize. When it is bid by a rival power, takers will be found among the morally, intellectually, and emotionally delinquent no more numerous than the indexes of very gross criminality and certain forms of acute mental illness would indicate.

Loyalty to Government

There is in this country deep and widespread pride in "the American way of life." The very hysteria about the Soviet threat is a misguided consequence of deep conviction that our democratic values are superior. There is a general if roughly formed realization that the claim to superiority is somehow unique, differentiated from the sense of superiority which would impose one's own judgment on others; that the superiority has no logic of exclusiveness, does not predetermine or impose other values than those of means which keep value questions ever open to those who use them; that these means are conceived in sympathy, tolerance, mutuality; that they offer to others every good to which we ourselves aspire or *might* aspire with no determination by us of what their goods shall be. In some such terms we have great enthusiasm about our country.

Fear of the future here is largely focused outside our borders. When expressed in domestic terms it generally implies high acceptance of the present condition and is otherwise indicative of no more than caution with respect to the unknown, and normal differences of opinion in a political and two-party nation. Here is no marked or general disintegration and therefore no lack of patriotism, no general lack of ethical concern. Our problems are in the complex equating of pluralistic values in concrete-action situations.

Even so there are governmental loyalty problems, some of them recently emergent, some as old as our democracy, and some as old as philosophy. Of the older ones, our intellectual difficulty turns chiefly on an inclination to make an absolute out of the right of dissent. It is true that loyalty to democracy is to a means for determining public values, that disagreement is implicit in democracy, and that disagreement over a long range of different possible opinions is not a test of loyalty. Yet the right of dissent has never covered treason or even some less extreme offenses. The right of free speech, similarly, has never licensed libel or slander (except for public officials!), and even the right of franchise is ever subject to legal redefinition. Nor can it be believed that the theory of democracy is so absolute as to deprive future generations of it if only one generation votes so to do. Espousal of an absolute so confining of humanity approaches the absolute zero in absolutes.

The older theoretical problem thus merges into the new, which turns on the rise of the Soviet Union as a great force committed to an undemocratic ideology, and the gradual but now conclusive demonstration that this force and all who associate themselves with it are so committed to hostile action as to constitute altogether a clear and present danger.

So long as there was no clear and present danger, and until it became plain that an American Communist sympathizer was required by his ideology to surrender loyalty toward the United States to a loyalty to another state, advocacy of communism could be tolerated as expressing just another variety of political position. A differentiated theoretical communist who favored American communism as contrasted with Soviet communism, a communism democratically achieved and maintained, still would be so tolerated. Even now, we go farther by still tolerating the Communist party. Except for applying laws of long standing, we have done no more than make the governmental employment of Communists illegal. This is in line with familiar moralities of the sort that in private fields would mark as a hypocrite a prohibitionist who engaged in the liquor business, or in public fields would similarly identify a judge who violated lawlike standards of the legal profession. Such hypocrisy in public responsibility is the height of the venal. Senator Joseph R. McCarthy is the last of the kettles who should call the Red crackpots black, even though responsible citizens must agree that Communists can no longer be tolerated in public employment. Where the informed must disagree is with McCarthy's irresponsible and unsupported allegation of the widespread character of such employment, its importance, and administrative failure to deal with it. He has damaged the government generally, and he has damaged its ability to deal with the particular problem. It was a notably superior morality which caused seven Republican senators, led by Margaret Chase Smith, to denounce and repudiate the McCarthy tactics.

In the sense of Senator McCarthy's attack, disloyalty to the government of the United States among its officials is no more of a real problem than are insanity and gross criminality, which occasionally are found. Nor can a congressional investigation ever hope to deal constructively with its identification. This is true for the same reason that one could not expect Congress to deal constructively through similar means with the identification of insanity, or with theft or murder among government employees. All these things are inevitably to be dealt with administratively, and the proper function of Congress with respect to them is to control standards, penalties, and procedures, and to fix, scrutinize, and work through, points of administrative responsibility. Loyalty within the executive branch in its very nature is an administrative matter, just as loyalty within the legislative branch is inevitably a congressional matter.

A brief approach to the consideration of loyalty in administrative terms might be found in treating the related problem of "security," which for some strange reason is readily left by Congress to administrative treatment. The loyalty investigations reflect concern about security, but have been conducted solely in terms of loyalty. "Security" in its ordinary application has to do with custodianship, commonly exemplified in the watchman function but extending from protection of property to protection of work material, operations, and information.

In these terms security is a common and for the most part routine concern of administration. Two somewhat uncharacteristic but illustrative examples may be cited. One involved the security of civil service registers. The other had to do with what was believed to be sabotage on an experimental farm.

A number of years ago a civil service register was stolen from the office of the Civil Service Commission. There was reason to believe that it was sold as a mailing list to a firm engaged in direct-by-mail advertising. The misuse of it was a blot on the integrity of the civil service operation. Aside from efforts to recover the register and locate the thief, the incident turned attention to security measures designed to make repetition unlikely. Almost any new protective device involved heavy direct expense and heavier cost in more complicated working procedures. One proposal was to post guards at entrances and to admit to the building only those with passes, a procedure always distasteful to citizens. In a matter of this kind the proper administrative course would be to take all reasonable steps of not too aggravating and costly kinds, minimizing the risk but refusing to give way to panic and disproportionate efforts.

On the Beltsville (Maryland) Farm of the United States Department of Agriculture—a tract of almost fifteen thousand acres broken up into many fields and occupied by various establishments of six bureaus—experimental dairy herds in widely separate fields and barns simultaneously developed virulent tuberculosis. Department veterinarians were convinced that this could have occurred only as a result of intentional sabotage in putting laboratory cultures into the various drinking fountains. There were in the area a half-dozen laboratories whence the cultures might have been taken because of inadequate laboratory security arrangements, and two or three disgruntled former employees of the farm were identified. These items gave partial substantiation to the sabotage theory.

New security arrangements for the farm were considered.

The highest possible fence with spiked and slanting top was priced and found extremely costly for so large a tract. It was pointed out that a determined person could scale such a fence on a dark night at any one of many remote points. Even the limited usefulness of the fence would depend upon a patrol system, the use of guards at gates, and limiting admission there to those given official passes. This would have involved eliminating the public-educational aspect of the enterprise. In spite of the fact that the infected dairy animals represented a heavy investment in experimental work beyond their value as individual animals, it was concluded that the actuarial risk of some repetition of the sabotage did not justify the large costs and program damage involved in the proposed security arrangements. Subsequent experience has supported that judgment.

These cases exemplify the security problem in its simple and familiar aspects. It merges quickly with the problem of organizational loyalty, which is in a public organization loyalty to the government. In time of war or international stress, and at other times in some agencies and program areas, good administration involves the same concern in terms of very great values. The security function in these intrinsics is the function of national security. Much of what is done in the specialized "security" aspects of national security is conceived in extremely pedestrian terms in a panicky psychology and through delegation to mediocre officials with small responsibilities and capacities, resulting in ponderous routines of small protective value. Even so, the essential problem is of high importance, and dealing with it at the highest levels is often characterized by imagination, *expertise*, and courage. This is particularly true in the fields—rather new to this government—of intelligence and counterespionage.

In the more routine areas of civilian and peacetime performance the various reviews and investigations of personnel and of operations constitute a large part of the whole area of administration. This activity has a great deal of security content related to the dependability of personnel and the quality of their work. Investigations of personnel in specialized ways apart from general administrative inspection and review are carried on by special investigating units of bureaus and departments, by the Civil Service Commission, by loyalty boards, and by the Federal Bureau of Investigation. Special investigations particularly concerned with loyalty in the terms of McCarthy's charges involve an outlay of many millions of dollars a year, a cost which, per case disclosing questionable loyalty, would cause any efficiency engineer to become hysterical. As one example, the record of F.B.I. investigations for the Atomic Energy Commission may be cited. It checked 150,000 persons for the Commission in the first two and one-half years of the life of that agency, at a cost of $200 each. The Commission denied clearance to 216 of these persons, and on grounds of expediency rejected 333 more. These 549 were kept from employment, therefore, at a cost of $5,505 each. From January, 1947, to May, 1949, the Commission granted 3,317 emergency clearances with only a quick F.B.I. fingerprint check. Only four of these were later dismissed on fuller knowledge, and they on gounds of "questionable associations." All such specialized security information is a small part of the total relevant information developed in the course of the whole administrative process. Altogether such information is vastly beyond the investigative and digestive capacity of a congressional committee. The handful of State Department records turned over to the Tydings' Committee proved more than the members could handle.

Security thus appears to be an aspect of the general administrative responsibility for capable work performance, reliability of personnel, integrity, and protection of government property and material. This large concern entails the development of vast information with many parts, and the development of systems protective of responsibility. Any breakdown justifying extensive, detailed, and continuing congressional inquiry would not be a breakdown involving the presence of some Communists in the bureaucracy; it would be a general breakdown involving the whole administrative process. Some members of Congress appear to have discovered the problem of reliability for the first time, and in the red flush of that discovery they have been treating it much too narrowly. Some professional liberals also have become confused, accepting the debate in the terms in which Senator McCarthy and his like pitched it, tending to discuss the "right" of Communists to hold government jobs as if that right were of the same order as, or even less limited than, the right of free speech. Actually, the notion of "rights" to public employment has been extended too far, and this extension has resulted in unnecessary damage to employees who should have been caused to resign for reasons less blighting than charges of Communist affiliation.

The fundamental importance of governmental performance is such that all presumptions as to rights of employment in it should be definitely limited and always under challenge. Yet Congress itself is the chief author of such presumptions. If any employee is one on whom responsible officials cannot rely—for honesty, loyalty in general terms and loyalty to the program in which he is engaged, and for ability to do well that which he is engaged to do—that employee has no real right to his job. The nature of his shortcomings, his previous record, the availability of an assignment for which he can be relied upon, and other factors essential to humane dealing and avoidance of vindictiveness or whimsicality need to be weighed in determining action in the individual case. Insistence upon overly pretentious and rigid procedures which involve the bringing of formal charges leads to a situation in which remedial action is not attempted unless the charges are of a flagrant sort. Insistence upon tenure as such and insistence upon the rights of veterans to employment are two other factors making administrative betterment difficult.

To recognize unreliability only in the guise of real or assumed Communist sympathies is to dramatize the fact that many handicaps have been put in the way of administrative responsibility. In the present state of the world, surely a Communist or Communist sympathizer is not a reliable person in his capacities for service to the government of the United States. But if it were possible to reassign, to exclude, and to remove any person found unreliable, the Communist question would be largely solved except at the level of counterespionage operations. This is a difficult practical perscription, of course; yet there seems little room to quarrel with the theory of it. Its use in agencies crucial to defense and foreign policy can be most readily defended. For the government at large the inference of the recent silly outcry —that anyone other than a Communist has inviolable rights to governmental employment—should be avoided by strengthening administrative responsibility in its concern for reliability and loyalty in terms both broader and more fundamental.

The actual effects of the McCarthy scenario and others similar to it are inimical to all of these values. Such performances undermine morale, diminish loyalty, deprive the government of the riches of varying judgments and imagination, push toward dead-level mediocrity, actually invite disloyalty, and serve Soviet ends by creating domestic and foreign confusion and impairing confidence. The priceless loyalty peculiarly appropriate to the United States is in a pluralistic unity which the McCarthys ignorantly and irresponsibly undermine. Testimony to that loyalty—or its absence—may be best revealed in day-to-day work in the judgment of critical associates in a politically charged responsibility under vast systematic review. Mud, indiscriminately splattered, is the product of McCarthy dredging.

SUBORGANIZATIONAL LOYALTY

The common problems of loyalty in the course of public administration are not derived from a lack of that loyalty which is patriotism. They inhere in a pluralism of values and in the limitations of any single moral criterion. They would be faced in any new acceptance of the prescription for evicting the generally or mildly undependable employees. They are faced in countless exercises of administrative judgment. Practices that do establish criteria and process are better than no standards; the search must be both for better standards and for better, more flexible application of them.

George Santayana once posed the problem in this way: "Is not morality a worse enemy than immorality? Is it not more hopelessly deceptive and entangling? Those romantic poets, for instance, whose lives were often so irregular— were they not evidently far more spiritual than the good people whom they shocked?" The weakness of this of course is that another example of irregular living—such as that of those associated in Murder, Inc., or in the licensed lawlessness of the Hitler gang—would point to insistence upon definite criteria.

It was a related but somewhat different question that Justice Oliver Wendell Holmes posed when he asked whether it might not be a gain if every work of moral significance could be banished from the law altogether. He was not suggesting that moral concern be abandoned in the enactment of law, and it is to be doubted that he would have answered even his own question in the affirmative. He was pointing to the function of the administration of law as morally subordinate to enactment. The dimensions of a moral problem must shrink for the most part to those of the level of responsibility at which it is treated. Those associated in an organization must substantially rely upon, and defer to, the other determinations of the whole and its parts other than their own. Loyalty to organization and its hierarchy does stand, for one of its members, somewhat in lieu of a hierarchy of individual moralities.

This is not wholly true, of course. It cannot be wholly true under any concept that dignifies the individual or any system claiming democratic character. The public official does not renounce the prerogatives of citizenship by becoming an official. Yet every degree of special responsibility everywhere qualifies prerogatives.

To some extent the qualification is associated with narrowing the range of choice and identification of true alternatives—choices within the limited range of the really feasible. Such narrowing and identification are functions of responsibility. A hundred million citizens may talk freely about a hundred million different conceivable lines of action, almost all of which are wholly outside the range of the feasible and mutually agreeable. Officials can spare no energies for such ranging.

Within the narrower range, moral problems are enhanced by the very responsibility which requires reduction in range. Matters arise in which officials cannot simply accept the values of their superiors. And even within the range left fully open to their individual responsibilities they have to equate different and unlike values. These necessities pose problems distinctly personal. They also pose problems of conflicting loyalties within the organization.

In one case an official may be so out of sympathy with the distinctive policies of a particular administration that he may feel in honor bound to resign. There may be many intermediate degrees of such disagreement; for example, he may be happy about his own agency and unhappy about the course of government elsewhere, or he may take violent exception to some single determination while generally in agreement with others. Perhaps the most frequent example is the official who, zealously concerned about the particular governmental function in which he is engaged, feels that higher officials with other functional responsibilities treat his function too restrictively. In such a case his trouble usually is parochialism, and wise counsel is that he should rely more upon the whole process of his organization and the general process of governance; this is the counsel of heightened loyalty to the larger and broader organization and to the democratic process.

An admirable and unusual example of loyalty in such a situation was provided by Katherine Lenroot when, as head of the Children's Bureau, she was confronted with a presidential reorganization plan involving transfer of the Bureau from the Department of Labor to the Federal Security Agency. The transfer called for some lessening of the identity of the Bureau and lower hierarchal status for its functions than had obtained previously. Powerful friends offered to start agitation which easily could have defeated the plan. Miss Lenroot refused to encourage such agitation, saying, "Any such action on my part would weaken a sector of the fabric of executive loyalty and responsibility, without which the Federal administration would approach impotence."

The loyalty essential to any organizational membership varies according to the purpose of the organization and its importance to members, to society, and to the public. Loyalty to the government stands generally at the head of any such sequence. It requires the normal bulwarking of substantial employee dependence on government pay for his own livelihood or full independence of rewards from any other organization. This argues generally against the use of dollar-a-year men or persons whose pay from private employment continues when they go into the public service, which usually involves a subtle personal independence modifying public responsibility. It requires bulwarking that comes from repute of public service and from a special concern for association with a peculiarly worthy activity— which is the decisive factor taking a very great many government employees into the public service. It requires the bulwarking that comes from patriotism, and especially a patriotism consciously devoted to political determination of value problems. While some public places may seem superficially to be quite like places in private employment, perhaps no one should work for the government who would regard the government job at the time as merely competitive in pay and working conditions with a private job. One important reason for this is that public personnel must be peculiarly disposed to see that many times their judgment of what is good must yield to the organization which is the vehicle for the public's pursuit of the public good.

The test of the loyalty thus sought is faced most often in the need for reconciliation of general policy and systematic process with differentiated actions in small-public, areal, and individual-citizen terms. Here the problem goes deep, to the nature of our government and its values. If there were complete and simple reliance upon determinations at higher levels, we should have an inflexible and unimaginative bureaucracy which would actually defeat higher-level purposes and needs. Imagination and discretion are required all the way down the hierarchal line. This requirement divides loyalty and carries ethical problems to every level.

Actually, the practice is so generally differentiated as to

strain frequently in the direction of insubordination, particularly in functional self-interest and in deference to special publics. Departments yield too little and too reluctantly to "the government," bureaus too little and too reluctantly to their departments, and specialists too little to the generalists. Suborganizational loyalty which is reluctant to yield to the larger organization is associated with the politics of special interests but often expresses itself in terms hostile to more general political determination. The reluctance of specialists to yield their special ground is even more frankly expressed in opposition to the processes of politics. In the one case there is a clash in political values, in the other the clash is between political values and non-political values.

These differences have both horizontal and perpendicular directions. Horizontally, they tend to an exclusively organizational character, posing conflicts between units and sub-units concerning functions and prerogatives. Perpendicularly, while having the same character they have also on occasion a quite personal content. An official is not inclined often to take highly individual offense leading to his resignation because of difficulties posed by units alongside his own. In up-and-down differences there is more opportunity for personal affront to an individual sense of responsibility; here is the boss-subordinate relationship, and in terms of this relationship here is focused the rather constant conflict between broader and narrower loyalties. Both laterally and vertically the differences are between the whole organization and its parts, between parts of the organization, between the individual and the organization, between individuals, and between values thus identified. The significance of the perpendicular relationship, however, is in its compression of such differences incident to its function as the peculiar and final vehicle of authority.

Rudimentary loyalty calls for adherence to the purpose of the unit to which a specific function belongs. This ordinarily includes personal following of the head of that unit, who symbolizes, and more or less incorporates, the leadership responsibility associated with that unit purpose. Normally, following the instructions of the unit head is associated with the sense of virtue involved in duty and devotion to a worth-while purpose. Apparent imperfections in leadership are generally overlooked in concentration on the larger values so long as the total leadership performance seems to support, rather than to detract from, the achievement of purpose. Mild dilution of instructions often enough is possible to make a supportable working situation. But sometimes imperfections in unit leadership may appear so crucial as to violate the values of the unit or those to which the unit values are organizationally subordinate. Both individual and group frustration may result. The group reaction is usually more impressive and effective than an individual reaction. In either case the first recourse is protest and the second is appeal. Manner and method are important in both, but since the group is relatively strong and the individual is relatively weak, manner and method of individual protest and appeal become particularly crucial. In both cases action within the organization—rather than by resort to gossip columnists, interest groups, or members of the legislature—is the limit of loyal practice short of some ultimate sense of wrong. Protest and appeal normally proceed, too, in steps of regular progression up the hierarchy or according to some condensed but regularized process of level-skipping. These are ordinary dictates of organizational morality.

There are extraordinary instances, however, in which level-skipping is proper. The case of the secretary of a certain official is recalled as an example. This young woman once brought to the office of the secretary of a particular department carbon copies of letters she had written at the dictation of her chief—letters which showed conclusively that he was campaigning vigorously in opposition to basic policies of his department. In great distress over her disloyalty to her chief, she recognized a superior loyalty to the department and to the administration. Her appeal to so high a level was appropriate to the case, less likely to be misunderstood and more likely to be effective than an intermediate appeal. In the same way, high officials are sometimes visited at their homes by subordinate personnel who come to report evidence of some financial irregularity. They are, and should be, invariably welcomed and protected against reprisals. In contrast, employees who go out of channels to report petty and distinctly personal matters reveal themselves as deficient in organizational loyalty, understanding, and performance. Loyalty to the more inclusive responsibility is prized, even though it does—as it must in some degree—involve disloyalty at a lower level. But mere disloyalty to intervening responsibilities earns no respect. Value judgments in these terms characterize organizational performance.

The most frequent form of this problem is illustrated in simple dimensions by "The Indonesian Case" in the casebook produced under direction of the Committee on Administrative Cases. For most officials comparable situations are complicated by the presence of many more relationships, making description much more difficult but at the same time making resolution of the problem more organizational and less personal. In the Indonesian affair only two persons were directly involved, in an isolated office. The junior of the two was a newcomer, qualified as an economist, assigned to the preparation of reports to the State Department on economic matters during the period of conflict between the Dutch and the emergent Indonesian government. The senior official, with caution or bias, instructed his junior to have no dealings with the Indonesian authorities. The latter, probably with a different bias, felt that this made complete and accurate reports impossible. After following instructions for a time, he determined to approach the Indonesians, did so, and filed a report making plain his insubordination. Cordiality between the two officials ended, but when the State Department expressed special satisfaction in his report, practice as determined by the junior officer became regularized.

In an isolated organizational situation the ordinary method of protest before acting contrary to instructions might have resulted in such a firm stand by the senior officer as to have increased the degree of insubordination his subsequent action would have involved. Appeal to a higher authority was uncommonly difficult and delaying. In a larger unit either protest or appeal might have been associated with the development of group judgments in a shared responsibility and wisdom. But sometimes the problem of a conflict in values felt to be important is inescapably personal, even though having great organizational involvements.

THE INDIVIDUAL OFFICIAL

Secretary of State Dean Acheson brought such a problem dramatically to public attention when he made his statements in the Alger Hiss case.

Concerning the Hiss statements, in the New York *Times* Arthur Krock summarized the judgment of one part of the public in substantially these terms: It is the duty of the Secretary of State to keep his office outside of unnecessary controversy; the former connection of Hiss and certain others with the Department of State had already hampered its effective operation by arousing the distrust and resentment of many worthy members of Congress and the public; the Secretary should weigh the effects of what his conscience as a man might prompt him to say or do against the consequences of these on the great public duty he had accepted. Mr. Krock also stated the opposite view held by another part of the public: "Personal, deliberate courage, loyalty to friends in dire trouble, and profession of the Christian ethic of compassion are admired and respected in Western and other civilizations. All of these were displayed by Mr. Acheson."

Perhaps no other modern case has so effectively presented to national attention the possibility of conflict between organizational and personal loyalty. Such problems in values face public administrators much more often than the public has ever imagined. Few men so appropriately as Secretary Acheson could have presented such a case for public attention, for few in our history have been so distinguished by either personal character or thoughtful and responsible concern for public morality. His criticism of a proposal is likely to turn on a question of legality, propriety, or "an unnecessary squandering of the nation's moral capital." He left his first post in government over a difference arising from his meticulous insistence on legal and constitutional qualms related to his professional qualifications as a lawyer, but of an order appropriate to his post, that of Assistant Secretary of the Treasury. In the urgent conditions of the time he was ousted because of presumed insubordination, but he made no public protest or defense and in the following election campaign spoke forcefully for the President who had discharged him, doubly demonstrating organizational loyalty in addition to his loyalty to personal principle. Further, while speaking to the legal point he never attempted to elevate the legal view over either the economic or the political, as a smaller person might have done.

Another attorney in the same position, for example, might have treated the monetary-policy question as involving violation of contract, in effect denying the capacity of the nation to treat the integrity of money as of a higher order than the presumed monetary contract, or the integrity of the economy as of a higher order still. Acheson took the most elevated ground open to an official especially sensitive to the discipline of law and deferred at the same time to other values. In the Hiss matter he again demonstrated dramatically an especially deep reliance on high standards of integrity.

It may be seriously doubted that Acheson's expressions in the Hiss case actually damaged our foreign policy or the conduct of the State Department's business. The "many worthy members of the Congress and the public" who criticized him may have been, on the one hand, timid, fearful, and weaker friends and, on the other hand, those already hostile and seeking excuses for attack. A good deal of the search for points of attack is implicit in politics and particularly in the two-party system, and its demonstration is often misinterpreted and its effects exaggerated. It may be that our leadership in foreign policy was made stronger by his action. The American people, and others, often have demonstrated great liking for such strength of character. In this country it often has been supported in elections in cases where it has been clearly evidenced and subject to popular vote. Even the appearance of it in somewhat counterfeit form has had great popularity. The dodging politician who tries to be all things to all men seems to succeed so often, perhaps, simply because he is of a type so much more numerous.

In any case the ethical problem was correctly stated by Krock. In the vast majority of cases, if the public interest suffers by insistence upon a personal standard, the action is wrong. Acheson would not consider, of course, bringing a man under a cloud into official responsibility, and even less would he bring, because of pity for him, one he distrusted to official position. But to fail in compassion and sympathy, or in courage to profess them, would have been for him such a retreat from principle as to challenge his own confidence in his ability to uphold a public trust. It is at the point where one loses his own sense of an essential rectitude that there can be no retreat with honor or with public advantage. The difficulty is in judgment about where that point lies in a particular instance. Some become so enamored of compromise as basic to democratic government that they lose all loyalty to everything else, have no good judgment about particular issues or problems, no real sense of how to compromise discriminatingly, effectively, or ethically, and are ready to vote for any candidate they would welcome to membership in a club. Others, less given to rationalization, reach the same end by abandoning themselves to compromising habits. Still others, in ignorance of how to compromise, will fight vainly for the impossible and the less relevant and yield a strong cause unnecessarily at the first hint of opposition.

Another vivid example of the conflict between personal and official loyalties was provided a few years earlier by President Harry S. Truman's attendance at the Pendergast funeral. Mr. Truman's elevation to the Senate had been at the hands of Tom Pendergast, whose political immorality was clear. Pendergast had only local political concerns, however, and wished, with respect to the national government, only that the opposition not name senators and congressmen. He, therefore, had asked exactly nothing of Truman. Truman, in turn, had asked no favors, had never even recommended any constituent for a job, and had built in Washington a reputation for official rectitude. He consequently had a feeling of personal—not official—obligation to Pendergast and gave expression to this feeling by attending the funeral when another man weaker in that kind of loyalty would have found himself too busy to leave Washington. Mr. Truman has demonstrated such loyalty quite stubbornly and not too discriminatingly, and the public has seemed to understand its meaning better than the information available would seem to make possible. If Mr. Truman had attempted to serve Pendergast's interests in his official actions, the judgment would have been quite different.

Somewhat similar problems face less eminent officials. When a colleague and friend is smeared by the Un-American Activities Committee, shall one cease to visit his office, have lunch with him, or visit his home? If one is financially or politically insecure or weak, personal loyalty wavers before the danger of guilt by association, even when the association is with someone in whose innocence one is confident. At the other extreme are officials who zealously build fences with the ultra respectable and the powerful, treating casually or even adversely the little men and the general public interest. Both tendencies have been much accelerated by the congressional witch-hunts. The Loyalty Board procedure, a defensive executive action, has been preventive of still greater congressional excesses, but the net situation has been a great diminution in the interplay of normal, highly valuable loyalties in the carrying on of public business.

The reconciliation and actual intermingling of the various values of loyalties continue, nevertheless, as important business in public administration. It is business of several dimensions, following a pattern of responsibility upward, downward, and outward.

X

POLITICAL RESPONSIBILITY

THE fear and distrust of government so extravagantly characteristic of the American people is attributable to many factors peculiar to our history. Fear of government has given currency and force to fearful clichés, counterfeits to thoughtful understanding of government, and many of these have caused citizens to regard as having precision and rigidity differentiations in responsibilities which cannot be made so definite. General differentiations in responsibility would be valid and necessary, even without the excessive requirements or interpretations of our Constitutional structure, but as often made they are so hostile to organic unity and real responsibility as to make actual operations unnecessarily and extremely difficult. The pattern of responsibility as it has been thought to exist may be confused by more realistic insights, but no valid pattern will emerge from the sharp pen strokes of geometric form produced by the strictly logical. Democratic governmental responsibility is in all its parts patterned basically in the supra-logical life processes of politics, better to be revealed through the composition of an artist in oils.

ORGANIZING POLITICAL JUDGMENT

The phrase "separation of powers" in becoming a cliché has been exaggerated, abstracted from reality and built into a firm and unrealistic dogma obscuring even while apparently simplifying the problem of responsibility. In turn, it has been overlaid with the phrases "quasi-legislative" and "quasi-judicial," regarded as actually, clearly, and finally defining certain aspects of the fulfillment of law. Similarly, the phrase "checks and balances" has come to have a sanctified value demanding conscious elaboration of structures opposing the needs and realities of the functional life of the political-governmental organism. We forget that the use of such phrases is analytical, not functional; it is as if the scientists who, separating a heart from a human body, and learning about the heart by keeping it "alive" artificially, should conclude that they in their *method* alone found "the" solution to "the" problem of life. There are, on the other hand, implicit in the general arrangements of government and in the functional life of the governmental organism, important but often quite different checks and balances, as good biologists and psychologists might readily guess. These have been too little studied. The orientation should be positive, to the organization of political-action judgment in a whole structure of political responsibility.

Federalism itself, conceived as a device for making the original union acceptable, is a system of checks and balances in a sense organic, in another sense artificial. The theory of home rule at the local level has provided a doctrine of analogous character within the states, bringing to a total of three the main levels of government, further broken down by multiplication of jurisdictions and special authorities for schools, drainage operations and many other activities. Division of the governmental structure at each of the levels under a separation of powers theory has added other checks and balances. Division of legislative bodies into two houses for two of the levels (and occasionally even for the third) has further checked the process of agreement. Executive government disorganized by long ballots and autonomizing procedures and responsibilities for its parts is a further development of the same pattern of checks and balances. "State rights" long ago became a symbol of virtue, "centralization" a symbol of evil. These are illustrative of many elements which make "government" here a term amazingly vague in meaning to its citizens, even causing some members of Congress to feel and to act as though they were not a part of the government.

Democratic aspiration within this very loose structure has reached variously toward many co-operative arrangements which divide and cloud responsibility. It has propelled us also toward means for "citizen participation" in the operating business of government without much uniformity or clarity of pattern, and without very critical concern for the feasibility or fairness of many arrangements. Often by such means special privileges are conferred without achieving the really representative and responsible performance intended. Private benevolent activities come into association with the newer public welfare functions provide one example of a degree of private control of public activities without public responsibility. Private–very private and self-perpetuating–organizational development into a pattern similar to the three-level governmental pattern as a kind of private federalism has added complications to the complicated intergovernmental relations of health, hospital and welfare activities. A special kind of citizen representational function thus has become recognized with real power but extremely fuzzy responsibility and inadequate representational character. Within the field of strictly intergovernmental relations there has been revealed by the studies of Professors Anderson and Weidner a distinctly professional interaction with its own professional sovereignty confusing to governmental responsibilities.

Yet government, like the rest of society, must utilize the fruits of civilization, bringing to bear on public action the whole relevant body of specialized learnings. This requires complex organization of government which is not necessarily the kind of complexity which was conceived for different reasons in general terms of checks and balances. It requires both within and outside of formal government many means for organizing out of the whole vast area of free and speculative thought successively more definitive and more truly alternative possible courses for actual action decisions. This is the central purpose of politics, but politics in the United States is lamentably little organized to fill the great gap between free, ranging, pluralistic thought and the responsibility of decision-making. There is little popular understanding of and orientation to decision-making. The burden falls precipitately and much too heavily on government without complementary organization of public opinion. Members of Congress, for example, fail almost wholly in that half of their proper role which is educational —the provision to citizens of adequate exposition of public problems and alternative possibilities as they come into focus within the government. Professional commentators, characteristically having little decision-making orientation, similarly help much less than they should.

Government is pre-eminently an institution—not merely the sum of many individuals associated apart from a peculiar structure; it is a special "culture" with its own history, processes and disciplines all emanating from influences rooted in its controlling environment. Democratic government to degrees elsewhere unapproached is dependent for its dynamism and its values upon its institutional responses to these environmental elements. Here, however, public sentiment tends to accumulate and take form slowly, and to become effective after the need has become acute, inducing spasmodic pendulum swings of governmental adjustment.

Formal government has as its primary function the furtherance and actual crystallization of the political processes pointing toward agreement on courses of action. Government as a whole is the last process in a long and complicated series of processes in which such agreement is achieved. The series is longest and most complicated for democratic government, in which the first process is an almost unlimited range of discussion. Between the two extremes, without adequate identification, organization and use of intermediate processes, there is occasion for vast confusion of citizens and officials alike.

Intermediate organization of the processes narrowing the range of choice identifying true alternatives and areas of discretion, has had far too little attention. Elections, of course, are a primary means, but elections apart from supporting mechanisms would be wholly inadequate. The instrument of parties emerged rather spontaneously—and here, happily, in a two-party form—but it has had insufficient rationalization and use. The sequential presidential nominating conventions have been on the whole the most important and successful of the more specific devices for majority decision-making.

A part of any organization of agreement-achieving processes is in the social and political patterns which determine who shall be effective, how effective, how limited and controlled. Patterns different from present ones would be achieved by changing Constitutional provisions, economic organization and practice, voting qualifications, party organization and performance, membership and functions, jurisdictional lines, representational patterns, etc.

In recent years administration has had disproportional and undiscriminating public attention, attention too much apart from consideration of private disciplines and private responsibilities, too much apart from the pre-administrative organization, disciplines and responsibilities of politics. These, of course, are closely related. Many governmental structures and methods have been inappropriately designed because too separately considered.

PRIVATE AND PUBLIC DISCIPLINES

Because democratic government is so extraordinarily political, it has a sensitiveness that continually causes it to lead in the advance of action organizations toward considerate and co-operative spirit and method. Only the universities may be thought to compare with government in this respect, and the action necessitates of universities are so much less than those of government as to make that comparison invalid. In the national government in particular, where perverting special popular forces tend to be subsumed in larger, common political forces, enormous effort is expended in intraorganizational co-operation and in building workways highly deferential to public and individual citizen values. The pattern spreads from and through democratic government to private organizations—not from private organizations to democratic government. We therefore see private organizations becoming steadily "more political"—more concerned with more various popular values, more considerate and less arbitrary. The area of personal privacy here is greater than at any other time or in any other state. Here there is more negotiation and less exercise of bald power in business affairs, size and power potentials of institutions considered.

It would not always have been possible for a Chester Barnard to say as he now truly says of organizations in general that "experienced and effective administrators prefer not to use authority." This social development within state and society here is a product and a byproduct of the democratic state, a fact sharply in opposition to the oversimplified notion that government is generally distinguished from other organizations by coercive character.

The theoretical emphasis on coercion as peculiar to government overlooks the wide range of influences and controls that govern human beings and the wide range of difference in government functions. The fear of coercion is most often vocally directed at the national government, which uses it less often and less consistently than state government, which in turn uses it less often and less consistently than local government. The number of arrests a year in a typical city exceeds 10 per cent of its population; at the local level generally, citizens are rather constantly aware of "the law" near at hand. Compulsory education, which touches most citizens most often, is a function of state and local governments. Not much resented, it is not unlike a good many other modern compulsions of government. So far as the national government is concerned, most citizens live out their days—apart from their involvement in national defense—without thought of the possibility of prosecution or onerous controls, even though respect for federal process is such that they exercise special care in those matters which do come within the area of that jurisdiction. The force of taxation—one of the most widely felt coercions—is not particularly subject to differentiation at the various levels, but the national government gets such bouquets as there are for a more complete systematization of a kind which mitigates coercion. Where the burden of taxation has greatest dimensions and complexity—as it falls on corporations and wealthy individuals—it is by assignment to managerial staff assimilated into the otherwise complicated functioning of large undertakings.

In its extremely limited exercise of the police power proper, in taxation, and in connection with national defense the government does have a coercive character perhaps peculiar. But these activities are not on the whole what is inveighed against. In considerable part the fear expressed is vague, general, and pointed toward future possibilities rather than present realities. The generalized fear of government ignores the large areas where primary administrative roles are to respond, to provide service and benefits, to educate, to persuade, and to induce. Misunderstood similarly is the government's capacity to influence affairs by general types of actions. It is useful to emphasize these aspects of governmental action as having moral character and as important in the value-oriented pattern of public responsibility. They can be made even more significant than they now are. They are induced by political controls centralized in the chief executive and the legislature, in contrast to specialist and functional control associated with sprawling autonomies. They are clearly to be differentiated from most private disciplines as the more responsible product of a wider and more truly representative system.

Actually, the most coercive elements most often felt by the majority of citizens are those that emanate from private life, many of them blind and irresponsible forces, illustrated by "the market," the cost of living, the level of employment and the impact of technology upon particular types of occupations. Economic practice, such as the custom of reflecting to individual purchasers differences in cost of units produced in quantity, are enormously determining of the pattern of economic enterprise; this particular practice, of course, much favors the large established buyer, penalizes the small new entrant into the field, and thus supports the growth of business in directions of size and power.

Many other private disciplines are involved in one's memberships in private organizations. Of these, the disciplines related to family life and occupation are certainly not least. Job and business disciplines undoubtedly restrict free political discussion much more than laws, sometimes the occasion for dramatic court action and an aroused public concern. The scurrying hordes leaving early morning subways, even in these enlightened days, have worried faces speaking a discipline much more wearing than those of time-clocks alone. Some of the worries, indeed, are not so directly related to the job as to the whole body of social custom and style. Keeping up with the Joneses is a dominating and life-pervading necessity for many, and in various forms it drives and lashes all of us. Women and children have looked to government for releases from some extremes of family disciplines, and workers have looked to government for new protections against some of the disciplines of their job situations. Indeed, one of the important occasions for governmental growth has been a substitution of governmental organization and responsibility for some of the less systematic and less responsible, and often less rational, forces of private origin.

This private area is familiar and deeply interwoven into habits of living, varied for individuals in innumerable ways according to function, location, status and interests. It changes greatly in time and circumstance, and on the whole is accepted not very consciously or critically, in spite of the fact that it is heavy with discipline. Every area of such discipline leaves unoccupied checkerboard areas of discretion and between the various private disciplines unorganized problems of relationship which provide a great and confusing burden upon individual judgment. Integration of civilization's complexity is for the individual related to his choices of memberships in private organizations, his choices of activities of highly personal sort and other activities within the organization fields, and some kind of rationale or philosophy. Integration of the individual in the larger concerns of society and public is also highly dependent upon political integration of concerns arising out of the private area.

A highly important haven from citizen confusion, therefore, is provided in government by the processes of politics
in achieving a satisfactory balance in the totality and relationships of disciplines, ameliorating the indirect consequences of private actions and their associated disciplines,
and positively effecting a sufficient over-all integration of
the complex and pluralistic scene. In our society government
is on the whole a reserved and ultimate vehicle for the
citizen, and would appear here to be less properly an object
of fear as government than as a vehicle subject to pre-
emption by special-interest publics, merely using governmental authority to underwrite coercions theretofore
private.

Fear of government in the United States has become
basically a fear of politics—the very hallmark of democracy.
One resulting tendency is to make particular governmental
activities subordinate to particular private disciplines and
forces, not widely representative and not publicly responsible. The basic plan of the Federal Reserve System was and
is to respond to a realized need for central banking controls
of money and credit by turning that public function over to
bankers, and it is only one of many examples of the tendency
to set up independent agencies and quasi-public organizations in a retreat from politics and public responsibility. So
far as the whole public is concerned, the coercions are not
less when that is the pattern, and the orientations of the
agencies are much less to the public service and much more
to distinctly private special-interests and parochial policy
than is commonly realized. Establishment of distinctly clientele departments and agencies apart from the so-called
independent agencies in the executive branch proper, a new
development in this century, has involved an important
movement in the same general direction, even while con-
ferring upon executive agencies a new but less than wholly

representative character. Bi-partisan nominations, as in California, and for judges, surrogates and school boards in many jurisdictions, provide other examples of the undermining of political responsibility.

The same tendency has been carried forward by an elevation of experts into posts of general public responsibility, normally subjecting the Public Health services to medical dominance, the Office of Education to the special interest of professional education, and so on. The tendency at the special-interest level is to go still further; to set up a Department of Education with governmental powers but an abrogation of governmental responsibility to a "board of education" selected by the private interest, a Science Foundation under the control of scientists, a Department of Health controlled by doctors, a bureau of cotton controlled by cotton growers, a grazing administration controlled by the cattlemen, a Wage Stabilization Board in which the public would have at most a theoretical one-third interest. The admitted necessity for more and more expert competence thus supports the distrust of politics and the drives of private interest to weaken public capacity to use government in the truly public interest. They combine to weaken the capacity of government to contribute reasonable integration and meaning to our pluralistic richness. We compound confusion with confusion, and are surprised that citizens become confused. The remedy is fatuously presumed to be in more checks and balances, or in clearer and more arbitrary delineations of functions so as to extend disintegration, or in more rigid procedures so as further to exclude the flexibilities of political responsiveness and so to limit the resources of the general public.

POLITICAL DISCIPLINE

These disintegrating tendencies are actually a political corruption of government of the same basic kind as the disproportionate influence on government of a gambling ring, a racketeer, a vice king, a heavy contributor to party who seeks and secures business at high price or who dominates particular governmental functions or jurisdictions. The fundamentally virtuous structure and performance of government are rooted in the capacity for whole-public control and in responsibility of government to the whole public. The prime virtue of democracy thus is in politics, and the degradation of democracy is in the failure to organize or in actual disintegration of political responsibility, yielding public interest to special influence. The most important failings of public administration are reflections of the political-bad in a weakening of the political-good. These failings are rooted in inadequate political organization outside of administration as especially considered, but some of the inadequacies are within the government itself, its basic structure and related procedures, some within laws determining party performance, and some within consequential laws determining administrative structure. Some are within the field of parties apart from laws prescribing their functions and procedures; some are within the field of citizen responsibility. We have on the whole not too much proliferation of private disciplines, but too many private disciplines are too irresponsible, too little attuned to the aspiration of political democracy. Even more pronounced because more fundamental are the lacks of enough political discipline and responsibility and of enough citizens consistently concerned about political responsibility.

It is necessary to identify this basic problem in order to

provide adequate terms of reference for the consideration of administrative morality. While any full discussion of it is outside the scope of the present undertaking, one example of political decay may be cited. No better single illustration can be provided than by quoting in full a syndicated column by Marquis Childs:

PUBLICITY TRICKS PUT TYDINGS' FOE ACROSS *

By Marquis Childs

WASHINGTON—If you were to look up quickly from the hearing table, you might for a moment think that you had seen the shades of the past, the gray shadow ghosts of another era. Clay, Webster, Calhoun, the great orators of the Senate, the embattled men of another age, they must be more than a little puzzled at what they are hearing. They believed in something; they had convictions. Nor is it necessary to go so far into the past to find men like George Norris, Borah, the elder LaFollette, Thaddeus Caraway, Carter Glass. Their contemporaries often thought them wrong-headed, stubborn, cantankerous. But they stood for beliefs, for a way of life, with certitude, with passion, with heart and soul and mind.

The lengthy testimony of Jon M. Jonkel, public relations expert, is something new in American politics. A study of the transcript of that testimony shows that Jonkel, while he is too adroit to say it, might have boasted that he had created a United States Senator. He took an almost unknown "commodity," to use his own word, John Marshall Butler, and by skillful use of all the tricks of publicity he put him across against veteran Democratic Senator Millard Tydings.

Jonkel testified that when he came from Chicago to take over the campaign in Maryland scarcely a thousand persons had ever heard Butler's name. It is a remarkable story that he told not in any immodest way but just as a skilled operator describing how he turned loose in behalf of a new product when the market was right for that product. Here is Jonkel describing 20 and 30-second spot announcements on the radio:

* Reproduced by permission of Marquis Childs and United Feature Syndicate, Inc.

".... We used that in little jingles, something like they use for Bromo-Seltzer, 'Be for Butler, be for Butler, be for Butler, be for Butler, be for Butler, be for Butler.' And then end up with, 'Be for John Marshall Butler, United States candidate for United States Senate, Republican candidate for United States Senator.' "That is the kind of thing we were doing. . . . We had machine-gun fire, we had mortar shells, we had a ricochet sound, 'Bowie,' and things like that, and something to the effect of, 'That is the way the war in Korea sounds.' "

The jingles were worked out, according to Jonkel, by "a very competent advertising agency." They were played before and after each of Tydings' radio appearances in the last days of the campaign. While Jonkel was coordinating the publicity and advertising in Baltimore, Butler was being hustled about the state. This is Jonkel's testimony:

". . . We would have to dictate part of his releases and part of his statements over the telephone to him. He followed that day in and day out across the state.

"We, in the office, coordinated that caravan. We, in the office, did the releases on what he was going to say on the caravan. We had the contacts with the politicians, one, two or three days ahead of him. We had contacts with fraternal groups and business groups and everybody we could get to listen to him."

Jonkel had carefully studied the approach. He had made a personal survey of what people were feeling. He found approximately 70 per cent really didn't know whether Tydings had or had not done a good job investigating McCarthy's charges of Communism.

So, in the phrase of the public relations expert, here was an area of doubt. Jonkel almost single handedly set out to exploit that doubt. He did a superb job.

In his testimony he said his "salary and maintenance was to be $1,250 a month." If that is all he got, then he was woefully underpaid. Toward the end of his story to the committee, Jonkel summed up in words that, if they are true, can serve as a neat little epitaph on the grave of the American political system as we have known it:

"I don't think anybody really cared. 'Is it yes,' or, 'Is it no.' That is the real issue. I didn't believe anyone cares whether Senator McCarthy is right or wrong, and by anybody I mean the voters, the voters in Maryland. I don't think there was any big issue about which was right or wrong. . . ."

Here is a clear and frank exposition that it is the slick trick, the quick buck that puts over the commodity in politics as in everything else. The package couldn't have been improved on. Handsome facade, eminently respectable, good family connections. And the name, John Marshall Butler (shades of that great Chief Justice)! But apparently inside the package there were only old torn-up copies of the Chicago Tribune and some left over sound effects. Bowie . . . Clay, Webster, Calhoun . . . zowie!

Mr. Childs' column has significance far beyond the political depravity practiced in one election in one state. It points to a vast and varied failing in our attention to the problem of responsible politics, a failing at the popular level, at the party level, and at the congressional level. Such failing cannot but color the more specialized administrative process. The direction of reform is not to escape from democracy, not to flee politics, but to set about the continuing business of making not government alone but politics too, more systematically responsible.

Much citizen frustration in which administration is a target arises from imperfect political arrangements which condition administration. Our poorest governmental performances, both technically and morally, are generally associated with conditions in which a few citizens have very disproportionate influence. The determination of what are the politically effective publics and what is "the public" is crucial, and this is a problem of political organization, activity and responsibility outside the field of public administration proper. It is a problem raising important questions about the representativeness of the especially influential in particular jurisdictions, in party performance, and in interest groups as they affect formal government. It raises also some important questions about the procedures and the representativeness of our formally denominated representative bodies, too often parochial rather than truly public in their responsibilities. Public administration is one of the political processes of governance, with some areas of discretion peculiarly its own yet thoroughly dependent upon and interacting with all of the other political processes. Some of the most important improvements in public administration are dependent upon improvements in the other processes and structural arrangements for them.

The people of our society have more diversified and wide-ranging attitudes on public questions than any other people. Our government may reflect the attitudes of a larger proportion of its citizens than any other government. It certainly reflects a greater number and variety of citizen attitudes than any other government yet achieved. We fall far short of the ideal, however. In some other respects there are very great, and too little recognized, failures to realize our present intentions and pretensions. In some of these matters we lag far behind other democracies.

The Negroes here as a body have much less influence, and much less weight at the polls, than any other group of equal numbers.

Social conditions and political and electoral requirements and practices combine to make the poorer citizens probably not more than one-fourth as influential as their numbers would justify.

Very many—not merely in the South—are effectively disfranchised in one or more levels of government by residence in single-party jurisdictions. Many others are disfranchised by residence and registration requirements and by lack of absentee-voting facilities.

A very great many have little or nothing to say about the

nominations of many candidates. In New York State, for example, in spite of the existence of primary elections, single slates are determined by party organizations, and by custom in many parts of the state the very names of party committeemen are kept secret. This particular custom is as flagrant a denial of popular equities as the South has ever provided.

Party structure is so ill defined, party functions are so little and so unsystematically developed, as to give minimal content to party responsibility.

In many local jurisdictions government is the informal private property of a few strong and active persons.

In the whole pattern of political effectiveness thus formed, policy is not often a reflection of the real balance of popular political attitudes and aspirations. It is a product of the politically effective. The product is not often enough an abstraction of the position of a *majority* of the politically effective as modified by responsible leadership—always a factor in effectiveness. It is too often a complex combination of special-interest, minority policies, moderately influenced by responsible over-all leadership. The minorities thus influential are too often and too exclusively minorities of economic or sectional interest.

The area of discretion open to leadership varies roughly and generally according to intimacy and extensiveness of the direct involvement of particular policy and operations with the pattern of political effectiveness. This fact leads from consideration of political responsibility back to the more particular field of administrative responsibility.

The different degrees of administrative involvement in the political pattern I have discussed elsewhere at some length.* These usually reflect program differences in popular exposure or structural remoteness from the central chain

* In *Policy and Administration,* University of Alabama Press.

of command. Only two agencies of the national government, I think, for any other reason operate outside the general administrative pattern to be given summary description in the next chapter.

One of these in the Federal Bureau of Investigation. Somewhat nominally a part of the Department of Justice, several successive attorneys general have confessed privately their inability administratively to control it. Congress yields to it an extraordinary and extravagant deference. Alan Barth in *The Loyalty of Free Men* has identified the F.B.I. problem, chiefly in nonadministrative terms, with penetration, eloquence and fairness. As a national police agency new to our government in the last few decades, it is the least appropriate candidate for a halo, in spite of its valid achievements and able personnel. Much of the reform needed with respect to it would be effective only if made in administrative arrangements, but in the climate of recent popular and congressional opinion any considerable reform is probably beyond the strength and courage of administrators.

The second agency deserving of special concern, the Department of Defense, poses the same fundamental problem in part because of its limited exposure to and dealing with the populace at large. In part, however, the problem inheres in the special importance and power attaching to it, and therefore was recognizable by framers of our Constitution. Perhaps no other single thing is so essential to preservation of democracy as continuance and complete reality of civilian control of the defense establishment and its members. This is a difficult and enduring problem, solution to which is by no means ensured by mere retention of the Constitutional provision. That provision can be made meaningless by either congressional or administrative practice, or by popular attitudes elevating military heroes above civilian, political officials and controls. The high moral values of civilian control are in part—though only in part—dependent upon public administration.*

With all such general involvements in mind, then, we turn to a final chapter for an attempted summary description of the pattern of administrative responsibility through which administration seeks continually to nurture moral values peculiar to, and unfolded by, political democracy.

* I have discussed this problem at length in an essay constituting part of a symposium published by the University of Chicago Press under the title *Civil-Military Relationships in American Life.*

XI

THE ADMINISTRATIVE PATTERN

FOR the purposes of this discussion, the administrative pattern of responsibility must be described as within existing social, political, and Constitutional structures and procedures. We begin by accepting democracy itself as the basic means by which values will be indentified, pursued, and kept in moving balance. We accept for the present the conditioning social and political mores and structures and look within all these for the somewhat specialized pattern of administrative responsibility. This pattern in turn we relate to four central concerns. However these concerns arise, however they are compounded and proliferated in differentiated problems, they seem rather clearly to be essentially these: concern for the maintenance and development under modern conditions of a capacity for popular controllability; concern for method, manner, and equities humane and considerate of persons; concern for utilizing and nurturing an advancing, pluralistic civilization; and concern for the provision and exercise of responsible and unifying leadership.

Administration thus is viewed as itself requiring a pattern of responsibility. The requirement is for, and the reality generally and crudely at least is, a pattern subtle, flexible, and differentiated in its attenuations but firm at its axis, a pattern notably at its axis and variously at its attenuations involved in the larger pattern of politics and governance. This chapter attempts to bring together in summary the main outlines of the smaller, administrative pattern as it exists. It begins, of course, with the individual official.

The Individual Official

If our concern with moral performance were to take the exclusive form of insisting upon moral quality on the part of all individuals engaged in the public service, we could not thereby ensure the quality of performance we had sought. It is also true that if we had the most admirable system of organized performance, but permitted it to be operated by the weak and corrupt, our system would produce very inferior performance. Individuals with moral purpose and strength are important, and systematic organizational structure and processes in support of moral performance are important.

For many of the elementary values in human performance, assurance of satisfactory action may be reasonably obtained by systematic protections of the individual against weakness. Techniques of administrative rectitude in these terms are highly developed in the national government, the larger states, and some of the larger municipalities. These techniques are designed to prevent the "moral overstrain" treated by George W. Alger in a book bearing that title written in the days of Theodore Roosevelt, who was perhaps its most eminent reader. Practices systematically preventive of venality merge into the "red tape" seen by Sir Henry Clay and many other observers as peculiarly necessary in government to ensure the higher values of fair dealing, reviewability, and responsibility. These in turn tie into the disciplines of social custom and popular expectation which provide both a part of the individual's moral capital and much of the environmental restraint governing his conduct. These restraints and procedures in turn tie into the movement of governmental business through hierarchies representing formal vestings of responsibility, into the interaction of units and agencies variously concerned, and into interactions with citizens in the context of all these and the collateral factors of popular politics and popular control. Through all the process, the character, the competence, and the aspiration of individual officials remain everywhere important, although limited, factors.

Aware, protective, and responsive with respect to multiple popular attitudes, the official must be concerned with the business of organizing for and identifying successfully narrower alternatives susceptible to public acceptance. His own ranging thought must be gathered toward the focus of action need, and his own free expression must be substantially confined as an intraorganizational contribution.

The official therefore must guard his social life, carefully avoiding involvements which would provide him, even unconsciously, with the preoccupations or obligations clouding his abilities to make proper contributions to public-institutional judgment. If he should choose a friend for a working associate he must be confident that he does it because of the reliability and working effectiveness of the relationship, not as a favor to the friend. To a distinctly uncomfortable degree he must make work relationships impersonal. This includes, of course, the avoidance of hates and vendettas and clique memberships which would confuse his judgment, and of any tendency to judge intrinsics in terms of his own self-interest. He must be sensitively quickened to imaginative perception of the attitudes, interests, and meaning of those with whom he deals, deeply concerned with the craftsmanship of organizational effectiveness, flexibly and ingeniously searching for the highest possible point of feasible agreement. In loyalty he must, almost invariably up to the point (in rare cases) of his resignation, and usually even after resignation, work within the responsible disciplines of the organization. This is part of his special role on behalf of the public.

Even within such confines, even as merely one participant in a great organization, the burden of discretion is very great, the opportunity to contribute and to be felt indefinably wide. The manner and the means of supporting one's convictions, including inventiveness in perceiving how high ground may be held, are one measure of skill in the administrative process. Recognition of one's own limitations as only one participant in an institutional process provides both confidence and solace. In such recognition one may strive hard in support of one's own view, knowing that it will not be accepted unless it withstands the critical appraisal of many others, knowing also that any present judgment may be later altered. And in such limitations one knows himself to be responsible not for the whole action but only for his contribution to it; he need not often deeply regret the action if he regrets not his own contribution.

The end product is, and should be, an institutional judgment,* many of the elements of which derive from the public scene. The necessity for institutional judgment is the chief protection against definitely bad performance, although of itself it may invite performance at the common-denominator level of mediocrity. For positively superior performance, dependence rests first and most on public-political dynamism, and second on the aspiration, imagination, inventiveness, and skill reflected in the leadership contributions of individual officials to the decision-making process. Some of the skill may be expressed in general contributions to organizational form and method designed to protect and maximize the superior contributions; this is

---

* It is much to be regretted that Graham Wallas did not live to complete the second half of his book *Social Judgment,* which would have dealt with this subject.

a specialized form of the common element in leadership identified by the sociologist Homans in *The Human Group* as "origination of interaction to which members of the group respond."

The manner, spirit, and means characterizing an official's work, when they are generally characteristic of personnel, become a part, although not the whole, of the manner, spirit, and means characterizing an organization. The attitudes of personnel are not automatically translated full-blown into institutional procedures. The translation requires a special inventiveness, and is full of difficulty. But individual attitudes do so penetrate and pervade institutional attitudes that no one can find the line dividing them.

Manner and Method

Courtesy and tact are the rule in politically sensitive agencies, as with politically sensitive individual officials. They are less common in the politically inexposed and excessively secure jurisdictions and units. The desire to please may lead to weakness, special favors, and corruption, but in a disciplined and responsible public organization it stimulates a search for considerateness coupled with propriety. This search points to developing techniques and to imaginative interpretations of responsibility which mitigate but do not nullify the intent of public policy.

A few laws—preferably a very few—are enacted at all levels of government to identify goals rather than to be speedily carried into action. Educational administrative action, as contrasted with enforcing action, is, then, the appropriate process. The New York State law requiring nondiscrimination in wage rates of men and women has been so regarded by Governor Thomas E. Dewey; its administration has been a matter of publicity, conferences, and admonitions. As practice develops, stricter enforcement procedures will be used, and without general offense. At the borders of purpose reflected in many other enactments are features which may be regarded similarly as calling for educational action and experimentation. As general practice becomes standardized, it loses coercive content except for those who strain at general practice.

Associated with operations of a more conventional sort, more and better educational activity in the course of administration would make for better results. In many areas citizens need more information rather than more enforcement officers. For example, it was found possible to provide information about plant and animal quarantines to passengers taking planes in Puerto Rico so they might be certified without enduring the nuisance of inspection and delay at the Port of New York. More interpretation of administration as a function in informing the public would translate some governmental actions from a coercion into a service. Legislative restriction of information-office activities, hostility to popularized reports as expensive, and executive specialists' inability to communicate in nontechnical language (including nonlegalistic language) make the government appear more arbitrary than need be. The lawyer-written jury summons, for example, seems everywhere to be more threatening and arbitrary than the treatment received when one responds to the summons. Familiar signs reading "U.S. Government Property—Keep Off!" provide another example of the unnecessarily offensive.

Identification and invention of ways in which to exercise general controls that leave individuals largely unaware of restriction can be carried far. The capacity to exercise general controls exists often in an ability to fix direct incidence of governmental action at a relatively few points, such as the banks, ports, and manufacturers. Importers long have served as collectors of taxes paid later by citizens as part of the market price. Incidence of a governmental action may rest rather heavily on citizen units thus become informal public agents, but the burden on them, beyond the dimensions of a nuisance, is not really borne by them, while the public nuisance of the action is minimized. In another dimension, general fiscal policy is often more easily effective and less burdensome than precise individual controls designed to secure the same result. By and large, general controls are more virtuous—less coercive—than precise controls, which should be resorted to only when general arrangements cannot achieve the purpose sufficiently.

Because of a central capacity for control—wherever that capacity is real—administrative decisions have a tentative character inhering in their revocability. A realization of this tentative character of decisions will be reflected in administrative manner. Some decisions—as at the flood site or the battlefront—do not have this character, but otherwise it is salutary as well as in accord with fact to realize that public administrative decisions in peculiar degree are subject to subsequent modification and betterment. This may occur in review before promulgation or in the light of learning in experience with their application. The capacity for review and modification thus penetrates the normal conduct of public administration with an importance beyond its exercise. It tempers, and should temper, the tone and manner of decision making. Revocability of decisions, rooted in central power of review, thus enters into the pattern of responsibility in a way having much public importance.

Some persons seem never to learn that a recommendation is not a final decision except as a decision to recommend, and that such decisions are modifiable. Fewer seem to learn that a decision reached at the level of presumed finality but not promulgated is not in fact a decision until it is officially released, and even then is subject to later modification.

Bureau chiefs have been known to argue that an old memorandum signed by "The Secretary" makes it impossible for the secretary to sign a memorandum taking a different position.

Tentativeness of action is associated with confidentiality of action in its preliminary stages, a condition which poses peculiar ethical problems of its own. All public business except that having to do with national security—and it in essential outlines—must be from the time of promulgation public, with adequate records subject to scrutiny. The public nature of this business, however, tends to confuse many who participate in it. Consequently, it is often discussed in a way which would horrify all accustomed to the disciplines of private organizations. A good deal of such discussion comes also not from recognition of the public nature of the business but from irresponsible disregard of reviewing prerogatives and one's own limited role.

The tentative nature of almost any executive "decision" is associated with special problems of honor involving presumed promises. The breaking off of a promise, when actual, is likely to arise in a misconception of authority on the part of the official who made it. More often misunderstanding is on the side of the person to whom assurances were given; he tends to exaggerate the meaning of such assurances. They can mean, as a rule, only such things as these: "It is my present intention to recommend," or "What you say sounds persuasive," or "I shall certainly see what can be done." Government officials on the whole have less power to make binding commitments than is generally understood. (Individually they have less power of any sort than is commonly recognized.) The matter of official assurance is peculiarly difficult since the tentativeness of executive action generally is associated with governmental viability. Viability is a principle, but it sometimes may approach or seem to comprehend violability.

A President may say to a job seeker that he "is going to appoint him" to a certain position. Whether or not he so assured James A. Farley, who wished to return to the government for war service after an earlier break with the administration, President Roosevelt did intend to appoint Farley; he made a good many efforts but discovered nothing "big enough for Jim." Was that failure a broken promise? In another case, having given assurances, a President may get information reflecting unfavorably on the applicant. Should the job be proferred? In still a third case the information might be that confirmation would be bitterly opposed in the Senate and would make other public business much more difficult. Should the nomination be made?

Presidents are particularly susceptible to misunderstanding about "promises." Even the reasonably sophisticated citizen exaggerates the power of the President, sometimes accepting as binding some assurances that are dependent upon the enactment of legislation, and invariably accepting presidential "agreement" as not subject to veto by an agency head, which it often is and often should be. Further, the interested person is never inclined to allow for changed circumstances. Perhaps each President is charged rather frequently with breaking his word in the early stages of his administration, before he has come to realize the degree of importance and finality presumed to attach to his most casual expressions of sympathy or agreement. The President's power symbolizes, but is itself subject to, the right of review. He is limited not merely by the public and by the Congress and by the courts; he is limited by his own staff, by his span of attention, by his responsibilities downward, and by his dependence upon the complicated competence and prerogatives of the bureaucracy. The result is everywhere great caution, great care, unequaled in any other kind of organization.

The organizational conditions which restrict an official's capacity to make binding commitments thus support—as they restrict—responsibility in the public's behalf. They cut the individual's moral responsibilities to his finite size, but at the same time they provide him with the resources of responsibility, shared and channeled.

RESPONSIBILITY UPWARD

Beyond the individual and beyond matters of method and attitude, the pattern of responsibility is in the formal structure of the hierarchy of government. A considerable part of this hierarchy is provided by the administrative organization of the whole executive branch. Throughout the entire structure, in which the whole formal government occupies levels subordinate to the popular level of citizens, the pattern of responsibility begins in and crucially turns on loyalty upward disciplined by the sanctions of hierarchy. This is true in all organizations and in all governments. The distinctions of democratic government lie in identification of the public as constituting the highest level, in the political processes available to the citizens, and in the consequent political character of those who occupy the centers of decision-making responsibility. These key officials are temporary occupants of their positions, there on the sufferance of suffrage and tides of sentiment in a multiorganizational and individually pluralistic scene. Because these things are so, there are early limits to what is feasible in governmental integration and a certainty of considerable governmental inconsistency. Responsibility upward therefore stimulates and effects only minimal, if extremely necessary, organization of public policy in general-public terms, while at the same time it stimulates and upholds differentiated responsibilities outward to the public. Communications from members of Congress, the White House, and department heads to agencies in behalf of very simple citizens are frequent enough to testify convincingly to this less-well-known aspect of a concentrated political responsibility.

A few individuals in coming together to maximize efforts of some sort through group effort pay as the price of that maximization a certain deference to responsible leadership. A leader may be deposed, but if the effort is to continue and to have effectiveness he must be replaced. The weakness of many co-operative efforts has been an unwillingness to pay a high enough price for leadership and its accessories. The more complicated the effort, the higher that price must be. Even the advanced and enlightened complication calling for a complementary deference to members has still this price of appropriate leadership, institutional arrangements, and procedures; the dignity of man is unrealizable apart from the disciplines of organizations.

Responsibility upward poses the problem of conformity versus insubordination. There are degrees of what might be regarded as insubordination. At any level things must be done which could not have been anticipated, fully perceived, or provided for at higher levels. This is true throughout the executive hierarchy. It is true with respect to authorizations in law made by the legislature seen as occupying the level next higher than the whole executive. It is true of authorizations made at the public level regarded as next higher than the level of formal government. At any point in the public-governmental continuum uniformly literal compliance with instructions drawn in other terms at a higher level can be in fact the most evil of all possible kinds of insubordination, more difficult to deal with than sabotage or outright refusal of compliance.

It is in that general direction that the McCarthys of our history would impel us. It is to that which too specific, too numerous, and too rigid constitutional or legal limitations would confine us. It is toward that which nostalgia sometimes pulls us. There unimaginativeness would consign us. Concern for stability in institutional arrangements which fails to incorporate concern for adjustment to social variety and rapid social changes, and concern for due process which fails to see that a process not effectively up to date, extensible and applicable is overdue are insubordinate to the ends of stability and equity.

In strictly executive terms some such apparent insubordination as is involved in nonliteral compliance is invited and expected by superior officers. It is essential to the survival of those in higher places. The concentration of responsibility in complicated and manifold matters dictates it. The differentiation of actions and the proliferation of actions in discretionary terms below the competence of higher levels are crucial extensions of the higher functions. These things are not insubordination, are not encroachment on a higher authority, but on the contrary are fulfillment or execution. They are important contributions of lower levels to higher levels.

Somewhere between this and true insubordination is an area of discretion that is tolerable in terms of the higher level. No subordinate ever does anything in exactly the way his superior officer would have it done; some deviations represent slight differences in personality or in color and manner of action—and equivalent deviations would characterize actions of anyone who might replace the incumbent. Toleration for such deviations is one of the prices paid by superior officers for the utilities of organized effort. The idiosyncrasies of a particular subordinate are tolerated— even appreciated—so long as it does not appear that an alternative selection would make for appreciable betterment in the performance. So the higher ranking executive himself must be judged.

Peripheral to this area of toleration is another, in which concurrence of the higher official needs to be enlisted. Beyond that is the area of true insubordination, wherein action is hostile to basic dependability. Around a core of reliability there can be, and should be, differentiated action, differences in opinion, agitation, negotiation, persuasion, and appeal; in the end and in general there must be a certain conformity.

A part of the responsibility upward, of course, is responsibility for dissent and for the giving of information useful, even though distressing, to the level above. This is the responsibility in which yes-men fail. It was the responsibility in which the steersman of the *Missouri* failed; he said he "knew she was aground, but did not tell the Captain, because it's not my place to give the Captain orders."

The responsibility upward covers a balanced presentation of issues, including information about the positions taken by various units and officials concerned, particularly those in dissent, and about the expected reactions of various publics. Heads of agencies, not good administrators, have been known to present proposals to the President in sketchy terms concealing important issues, and to use his cautious instruction to "clear with Secretary X" to say to the Secretary, "The President wishes me to do this, but asked me to tell you about it." Executives at lower levels fall often into the same error and fall also in the confidence of their superiors. Sophisticated executives learn to prefer proposals that are submitted in writing. Physical necessity related to volume of business points toward this preference, but experience shows that the written word will be more cautious and dependable; further, a written document is readily susceptible to reference for complementary or competitive judgment.

Responsibility Downward

The responsibility upward, then, is to state a case fairly in terms of the higher responsibility, as insistently as one's sense of its importance and propriety dictates, and normally to accept the decision associated with higher responsibility as one's own. There is a corresponding responsibility downward, to welcome differing judgments as contributory to sound decisions. There is need particularly to welcome the judgments of those who have shares in relevant responsibility, avoiding the favoritisms that undermine responsibility, and in general to support subordinate responsibility. Some executives try endlessly to determine for subordinates what cannot be determined for them. Administration rests on a pattern of responsibilities which does not end at any level. Maintenance and development of that pattern downward is the complement of one's own relationship upward. Loyalty of personnel on lower levels is won by considerateness and fair dealing. There is no reason for any change in *manner* as one deals with the level next higher and then with the level next lower. The only significance in levels is the difference in responsibilities they represent. A good administrator defers to the decision of his chief when it is made, but argues it freely before it is made; similarly he invites free discussion by his own subordinates and makes a decision when it is his responsibility to make it. He simply lives up to his own responsibility in each case.

Maintenance of morale, calling for intraorganizational magnanimity as the twin to magnanimity in dealings with citizens, is in large part related to the responsibility downward. In these terms the problem sometimes is a conflict between the value of meticulous honesty on the part of government officials and the humane value of compassion. The tragic story of a certain meat inspector illustrates this problem. Late in the administration of Secretary Arthur M. Hyde, in the Department of Agriculture, an inspector was reported to have stolen some meat from one of the packing houses he visited on his official business. The matter was fully investigated, the report was verified as involving about ten dollars' worth of meat, charges were brought, and the inspector was discharged. A year later, early in the Roosevelt administration when mail had so deluged the White House that its handling had lagged finally by sixty days, the former inspector wrote a letter to the new President. In that letter he truthfully told his story, recalling long and serious illnesses in his family, impoverishment, and acute hunger which caused him to take the meat to his needy family. He told of subsequent deaths in his family and of his inability at the bottom of the depression and with a record of discharge from his governmental post to obtain any employment. He concluded by saying that he could manage somehow to live for another sixty days, but that if not reinstated by that time he would be forced to commit suicide.

This letter had been read at the White House simply to the point of noting that it concerned the Department of Agriculture; a rubber-stamp reference to that Department was made, and the letter reached, and was read by, an aide to the Secretary on the sixtieth morning after posting. The aide hurriedly called the Chief of the Bureau of Animal Industry, read the letter to him breathlessly, and suggested that the Bureau Chief phone to his St. Louis office at once to have that office get in touch with the former employee. When the Bureau Chief had an opportunity to speak he said simply, "It is too late, Mr. X; we received word of his suicide this morning."

For some reason never understood, the theft of meat by other inspectors figured in one or two disciplinary cases a year for the next few years. The offenders were invariably discharged, but with official soul-searching and meticulous efforts to mitigate the damage to the individuals concerned. The government cannot tolerate even petty thefts by those who represent it. Yet the government has an obligation to be humane. To serve both values involves that search for the "superior moral principle" which Chester Barnard emphasizes as the obligation in which there are most administrative failures. More precisely, it is a search for ways to reconcile conflicting values.

Responsibility downward is perhaps three-fourths a matter of upholding subordinate actions. Up to the point where an unsatisfactory subordinate executive is transferred, led to resign, or discharged, he must be generally upheld to avoid chaos and irresponsibility. Short of an actual shift, the elements of stimulation, guidance, and circumspect interference, which are always factors in responsibility downward, should be increased.

In the course of his work in the Federal Security Agency, Roy E. Touchet has formulated an interesting thought relevant to downward relationships. He presents, as a possible principle in administration, the idea that the only normal basis for modification or reversal of the action or recommendation of a subordinate is "information exclusively possessed" at the higher level. Touchet properly defines information in this connection to include and largely to consist of those things derived from relatively wide exposure and high responsibility. Ordinarily, it surely is true that the executive who simply substitutes his judgment for a subordinate judgment, when that judgment turns wholly on matters equally known to the subordinate, is following a practice that corrupts administration. One minor exception and one of great importance are to be noted, as Touchet recognizes. The slight exception involves simple correction of errors which would be accepted by the subordinate on grounds of technical fact. The large exception involves difference in responsibility. Even when the higher-ranking executive has no information not possessed by the subordinate, in cases where a different judgment seems to him really essential to his greater responsibility, he must follow his own judgment.

Public Responsibility

The responsibility downward, therefore, is for positive leadership, for stimulation, for support, for guidance, for morale, and for assumption of one's own higher responsibility outward and upward. The outward responsibility is first of all intraorganizational, a responsibility to peers having related responsibility, calling for lateral clearance. This clearance not only secures fair dealing and order but enriches the judgment and acceptability of the executive who seeks it. The upward responsibility is ultimately to the general public. The outward responsibility is to the public commensurate with the hierarchal level. Lateral clearance takes care of this in part, because of the representative character of the associated units, but the responsibility outward in program hierarchies also extends directly to some publics. Responsibility downward involves deference to smaller, more special publics. Responsibility outward is deference to, and integration of, activities in terms of various publics and a larger public altogether, tempered by the responsibility upward which carries deference to the general public. The individual's moral problem inheres in the application of his individual standards in this process of adjustment and deference to the other values represented by the hierarchy and publics thus associated with him. His is not often the difficulty of a lack of moral standards; rather, it is the difficulty of conflicts in individual and group values.

Leonard White in the administrative history of *The Jeffersonians* cites the conflict which arose in the Jefferson administration in connection with the obligation of customs collectors and attorneys to enforce the embargo in communities where public opinion was violent in opposition. There was, he says, some sabotage among customs officers, one official was discharged, and a few sought to resolve their problem by resigning. When an official is influenced by his own convictions as well as by his particular public, such a problem is doubly acute. Is an official's loyalty in a particular case to his own values, to the values of the public with which he particularly deals, or to his governmental organization, and in what admixture? A tempering of the administrative wind to a local shorn-lamb sentiment is customary and moral —up to a point—under a government devoted to pluralistic, democratic values. Individual official conduct shaded on the side of the official's own deepest ethical concerns also usually is feasible and favorable to general morality so long as these generally reflect elevated concerns frequently found in society. When the individual seeks to impose personal standards of a specialized sort—professional, functional, private interest, or idiosyncratic—loyalty to the highest level of his organization becomes a crucial corrective. In practice all of these elements interact, and the problem for the individual and for his superior officers becomes one of weighing the elements in the mixture.

The problem arises less often than is generally supposed in terms of an excessive deference to centralized power. From many years of observation the only examples now recalled, three or four in number, were of no real public significance but simply carried some organizational theories to an extreme in much the same way as congressional committees have considered consolidating all statistical functions. In these cases not power hunger but a too simple logic was the cause. With somewhat similar motivation Congress has killed a number of regional offices as wasteful, forcing back into Washington some business the administrators would prefer to handle in the field.

The general tendency is in the opposite direction. In myriads of ways the government is organized to involve mutuality, consultation, co-operation, persuasion, inducement, service, and benefits rather than to impose a centralized and undifferentiated power. Administrative, congressional, and popular sentiments point rather unwaveringly that way. With all the pluralistic values associated with these forms and methods, they confuse responsibility and cause the public to guess a good deal about which shell the pea of responsibility is under. Yet even in their most confused stage these arrangements are in the long run much to be preferred to those David Lilienthal has espoused under a "grass roots" theory exemplified in the Tennessee Valley Authority. His plea for regional autonomy for regions not politically organized is another version of many efforts to take politics out of government. Without corresponding political responsibility the plea is really for administrative and special-public autonomy. Without political responsibility the theory is actually hostile to the democracy it seems to uphold.

In practice T.V.A. has been so well led and its functions so desirable that it calls for little present alarm apart from theory. But other parts of the government not organically separated to the same degree are in practice somewhat too autonomous, not too much the victims of centralizing power. Congress not infrequently has further impaired responsibility by vesting it in subordinate bureaus. The general fear of excessive centralization as a concentration of power in one or a few individuals, to be exercised by them whimsically and autocratically, is largely based in theory held by amateurs in government and administration. The more sophisticated have it as particular concern for what might be sometime in the future and in some sharp change in political climate, or for what sometimes is in certain relatively small and restricted areas of government. In all its forms this fear is associated with the over-simplified and in many respects erroneous notion, earlier discussed, that government is pervasively distinguished from all other organizations by coercion.

LAW AND AUTHORITY

The individual official, his organization and matters of manner, and his method of acting all have a certain basic dependence upon law and the outline of authority drawn by law. But authority apparently so vested is probably never fully utilized, even though changing conditions may greatly enlarge the authorities as earlier interpreted. Action may extend to the utmost bounds of authority in a particular direction, or even exceed them, but on the whole much less than the entire, currently theoretical interpretation of authority will be utilized. Even in the quite specific and measurable matter of expenditures, the need to guard against unauthorized spending and the need to apportion funds into many parts for management purposes will inevitably leave many small balances. This roughly illustrates the whole matter, but it bears further explanation.

The power to discharge is never fully utilized; the power to hire is never fully used. Delineation of larger outlines of authority is essential to the exercise of a less authority with discretion, acceptability, and practicality. To read the Budget and Accounting Act would be to believe that the Budget Bureau has much more power than it has; to read the organic acts of the departments would be to conclude that the Budget Bureau has no power. The authority of the one impinges upon that of the other, and a working relationship identifies authorities of each in terms narrower than the laws. Actually, the working relationship is more determining than the authorities; these are limited not merely by conflicting authorities but much more by workways and attitudes derived from the governmental culture and the public scene.

It is probably a valid generalization that law invariably must vest much more authority than can be exercised in practice. Similarly, presidents and department and agency heads must be vested with much more power than they can exercise, even institutionally. It is important as a potential applicable in particular cases and ways, and as identifying the area within which responsible discretion may be exercised, but otherwise a theoretical listing of powers possessed by any official or the government at large is without high significance. It is what has been and is being done that has most significance, and the manner of its doing. It is much easier to list theoretical powers than to describe the administrative process; even professional scholars have produced little of such descriptive literature. In consequence, many fearful discussions of government have little realistic relevance and desirable reforms come more tardily than they should.

Restraints upon the exercise of authority are in some respects managerial. This is simply to say that many exercises of authority would defeat their own purpose, would not be either effective or satisfying to citizens or officials. Very wide authorities are also restricted in practice by appropriations; limitations of a financial sort compel a choice of activities among the many theoretically possible. Again, as already suggested, authorities are impinged upon by other authorities. But the greatest restraints are imposed by the necessities of institutional performance, group judgment, and the political controls which make public agencies highly sensitive to citizen sentiments. The basic limitations on the meaning of a law are provided in ways beyond the reach of language by the culture out of which and for which it is drawn. Cultural influences penetrate the administrative process in subtle and complex ways far beyond the power of courts to identify or require, even though the authority of the courts polices certain boundaries of the area of administration.

All these factors of restraint operate on individual officials and are at that point sharpened into a focus of self-protection which characteristically over a period of time shades from mild caution to extreme timidity. This, not bold exercise of power, is the pre-eminent characteristic of civil servants. Even so eminent a civil servant as the late William A. Jump would never have been described by his most ardent admirer as bold, or even as generally and constantly courageous; his useful judgments were phrased with extremely careful conservatism and in complete avoidance of the more novel and controversial policy questions. Perhaps only thus could he sustain effectiveness and survive the storms of forty-two years of public service.

Low-ranking individual officials, like their superiors in key positions, generally exercise less authority than is theoretically theirs. In various ways, however, many individuals exert influence in excess of their formal authority, although it is the rare individual who willingly assumes very outstanding responsibility and gives strong expression to initiative. Within the limits of the organization's willingness to act, there are only vague—and expansible—limits to the responsibility an individual may assume, depending merely upon the acceptance he can win. As Woodrow Wilson remarked, there is no law that prevents a person from making his job as big as he is capable of making it; and the dimensions of every job change with its incumbents. As Wilson also remarked, all who come to Washington either grow or swell. Those who swell remain rather briefly, and those who grow much in a balanced fashion exert influence proportional to the responsibility they assume, not at all proportional to their formal individual authority.*

Increased responsibility is assumed readily by the rare executive who, with willingness to accept responsibility, so organizes the handling of assignments already possessed as to make himself free to take on more. Since such organization of his job is possible chiefly through delegation, his capacity to take more assignments or by simple initiative to elevate his own effectiveness is without sharp or definite limitations, other than the temporary ones involved in mastering whatever he has before him. Responsibility thus precedes authority, and ever remains for individuals much more extensive and extensible than authority, always in at least some degree qualifying authority. This complements the fact that authority is largely institutional, even when personalized in key officials, and cannot in general be fully exercised by anyone for the reason that no individual—not even a Hitler or a Stalin—is ever identical with, or equal to, an institution.

Even when authority appears formally to be invoked in some directive, it is much less than the full authority possessed and commonly is merely a useful ratification by authority of an institutional judgment in which a great many

* It may be of interest in this connection to note that while serving for seven years as Assistant to the Secretary of Agriculture and in that capacity functioning as the principal executive officer of the department, I had, aside from a not-too-meaningful "job description" in connection with my appointment (never seen or directly influenced by the Secretary), no more specific authority than the right to sign the Secretary's name to requisitions for noiseless typewriters. This was the only definite and continuing delegation ever made to me.

have shared. In this ratification aspect it is more a technique of communication than one of authority.

Authority wears out under heavy use. It limits one's future actions to the bounds of the earlier mandate, thereby reducing discretion; it reduces capacity to develop supporting responsibility by delegation; it impedes the flow of work and frustrates him who attempts the use of more authority than is effective. These statements have most truth in society and institutions with most democratic character and context, but they apply even to the authoritarian ruler who, dealing with complicated matters, must delegate and must regard much of his theoretical power as a reserved capacity to intervene and determine.

An American radio commentator who left Berlin just before the joining of war between Germany and the United States told privately several stories illustrating the use of discretion by subordinates of Hitler. One of these concerned the commentator's request for a permit to visit the combat area then existing in and near the Maginot line. He submitted his request to the Minister of Information, who submitted it to Hitler. Hitler denied it. The reporter could not in good taste request frequent interviews with the Minister, but he did renew his request almost daily to a deputy official who knew, of course, of the earlier denial. After about a fortnight, the deputy in weary irritation said in effect, "Life is too short to be bothered so much about this," and wrote out the desired pass in disregard of the earlier adverse ruling by Hitler. Subsequent experiences showed this to be no extraordinary or intolerable insubordination; the deputy had acted within a range of discretion he knew as necessary and accepted.

The greatest limitations on the use of authority are institutional and contextual, subtle, pervasive, and altogether of dimensions much more limiting than the most specific words in the most formal vestings of power designed to limit those vestings. Power is much more important and effective when it is largely a reserved power, illustrated in partial and rare applications rather than in constant and complete applications. The power to discharge an employee is very real— devastating to an occasional employee and widely influential —but the power to discharge all employees or even very large numbers of them, is at most a theoretical one, the use of which would completely ruin him who tried it.

Power, then, is most effective when it is far from fully used. Constituting a reserve capacity, its application may be imagined in any and all directions; much used, it becomes visible very quickly as distinctly finite. The point was once made by a teacher of speech in discussing gestures. "Power," he said, "is most effective in a speaker who impresses an audience with resources not called upon. In gesturing, therefore, one should never extend the arm to its full length; only God Almighty can do that and still reach further. *You* must keep a crook in your elbow." It is a sound dictum for administrators.

DELEGATION AND REVIEW

Citizens delegate, the legislature delegates, the chief executive and all administrators delegate. It is the basic process by which the effectiveness and responsibility of an organization are enhanced.

True delegation is a step-by-step, level-by-level, downward assignment or assumption of additional responsibility, every such assignment or assumption being subject to review, control, influence, and revocation at each successively higher level in a centrally identifiable chain of command. No true delegation thus fails to be controllable and recoverable and generally involves no significant total diminution in the responsibility or authority of the delegator; rather, it enables him to exercise more responsibility with respect to more things, and to be reinforced by the added responsibility of those to whom he delegates. One test of his subsequent situation is in the fact that his own immediate superior holds him responsible in substantially the same way after the delegation. The superior officer may recognize some new area of deviation as tolerable, but on the whole such deviation in style of action would have been as tolerable before the delegation. For the total net results of that performance and all others for which he has been or becomes responsible, the delegating official is fully accountable. By delegating more, and generally only by delegating more, can he assume substantially more responsibility.

It is the fact that delegation involves no really substantial diminution in the responsibility of the one delegating that makes the practice difficult for many. It is the temperamental and intellectual quality which enables one to delegate effectively that vividly distinguishes a "good administrator."

Efforts to concentrate all responsibility in the law itself, to make it specific and its coverage complete, reflect the same inadequacies as characterize the poor administrator who is unable to delegate, seriously diminishing both responsibility and effectiveness.

Moral responsibility is confused and damaged by establishment of independent or quasi-independent agencies designed to report directly to the Congress, and by legislative vesting of specific authorities in bureaus rather than in the departments or agencies of which the bureaus are parts. Both provide examples of level-skipping in delegation, which is a serious breach of the line of command essential to responsibility. Similarly, courts, with little capacity for understanding institutional performance, enforce irresponsibility when their decisions turn on requirements for intensive personal attention to a particular action by the head of an agency rather than on requirements appropriate to his responsibility for his conduct of his institution. Practical autonomy of any agency or any subordinate unit—its isolation from the responsible and complete political complex—would provide proper ground for an adverse court ruling. Within that complex, constancy of *general* practices of review, guidance, and controllability is the test of responsible action.

After relative autonomy, the chief administrative enemy of responsibility is level-skipping. Information brought to an executive or a legislator over the head of an intervening official should never be accepted at apparent value and should never be the basis for action apart from reference of that information into systematic channels. Relatively mild, infrequent, and indecisive use of level-skipping confuses responsibility, but when it is continuing it wholly undermines responsibility. The most extensive governmental irregularity ever revealed to my view—and one which logically sheltered separate acts of venal character resulting in penal sentences for two subordinates of the major offender—was simply to be accounted for as the result of years of direct dealing between the head of a division of one bureau and successive Secretaries. The division head became unreviewable and uncontrollable by the head of his bureau because he brought real or imputed mandates from the Secretary. No bureau chief can be held responsible when his responsibilities are not deferred to.

The key to true delegation, then, is the maintenance of capacity to review and control at each upward hierarchal level, and frequent enough exercise of that capacity for it to serve as a policing sanction of pervasive significance. So-called "delegation" to an agency not organically involved in the hierarchal structure is not really delegation at all, but a divesting of responsibility. There must be a core of particularity in responsibility, that core related to authority and structured in hierarchal form. Responsibility can be general only as it has the implementation of hierarchy below it and as general responsibility is concentrated in another formal structure of responsible representatives of the general constituency. Responsibility thus is firmly rooted in formal representativeness—and that is a term as little explored and understood as "responsibility." There is a tendency to attribute too much representative character to special interest groups not actually representative or generally responsible. Tripartite administrative structures and quasi-governmental organizations are the most formal examples. The tendency is associated with the notion that democracy somehow requires such devices. But democracy, irresponsibility, and unrepresentativeness are incompatible.

Relative autonomy or actual independent-agency status, pseudo delegation, and level-skipping delegation, in summary, are chief examples of a vesting of effective power in excess of responsibility. The first great barrier to responsibility is legislative and executive incapacity and disinclination to delegate in an orderly fashion in a hierarchically unified structure. The second is a reluctance at lower levels to accept responsibility. Executives are continually in search for persons with initiative, imagination and willingness to assume responsibility. This fact raises important questions about the cliché which portrays as a universal the "edifice complex" of the power hungry. The seasoned public executive in a democracy grows less anxious for power, not more. The seekers of sheer power are a small minority who get hurt, and learn, or depart. The great majority of executives try simply to live up to responsibilities already assumed. Their effort may sometimes appear to reflect a drive for power, but it is rarely that; the appearance usually stems from a desire to do well what they are charged to do and to simplify the complexity of their assignments. This is to say that they are trying to be responsible, primarily in terms of their hierarchal status, which is the most formal and concrete identification of responsibility.

Aside from the fact that organization could not exist at all without having structure, the significances of hierarchy are primarily two: the identification of basic responsibilities as a core around which, and only around which, more informal responsibilities may develop fruitfully; and the provision of vital organs for the basic functioning of organizational life processes. A centrally developed and complete hierarchy is essential to that good administration which in legalistic terms is less richly termed due process. In the absence of any completely hierarchal structure for the judicial system, and in the tenuous representativeness of judges, legalistic due process depends too much on individual character and capacities of the judges. In the general administrative field shortcomings are more attributable to the fact that processes are more complicated and varied, are extremely difficult to penetrate in systematic study, and are only beginning to be opened up to realistic description and intelligent criticism.

Whatever the present state of administration, it seems clear that its development must build on understanding of hierarchy as the structure of responsibility. Hierarchy characteristically develops that institutional judgment which amateurs often see as possible only through the much less responsible and effective boards and commissions. Hierarchy in democratic government also inherently possesses potentialities for the easiest, most complete, and most flexible processes of appeal and review within human experience in the conduct of complicated action business.

The process works rather consistently, and on the whole too well, if anything, when criticisms of action are heard from coherent groups of any substantial size. In governmental jurisdictions where control swings readily from one party to another there is an extremely nervous sensitivity to criticism which tends to a concern for group support often hostile to the general public interest. This is attributable largely to the lack of sufficient political organization in the public scene, but inadequate integration of the government, weak and incompetent political judgment, and official timidity also are factors. The most common citizen criticisms of administration tend to support and to aggravate these very weaknesses, not to correct them.

The process of appeal works also, less consistently but to an impressive degree, for small groups and individuals. This is a product also of political sensitivity, but the vitality of the democratic ideology and the attitudes of many individual officials are important associated factors. In governmental organizations as well advanced as are most of the national agencies a surprisingly serious and consistent attention is given to all complaints. Many of them, of course, arise in ignorance, misunderstanding, and bitter prejudice, but they are regarded attentively as a part of the opinion complex on which government is so greatly dependent. Really cogent criticisms impress and haunt officials and agencies and propel them toward searches for solutions often extremely difficult to devise.

The necessity for systematic handling of a great volume of mail results in knowledge spread wide in the organization of criticisms received, titillating the tendency of coworkers or personnel in contiguous units to criticize and to pass up the line word of trouble in a particular activity. One of the most important of administrative learnings in democratic public organizations is to pass on to one's superiors word of citizen unhappiness before the news reaches them by other means. Not only mail but field reports as well provide material for a great intelligence system dealing with citizen criticisms. It may be reasonably asserted that no citizen or group of citizens comes personally to Washington with complaints about widely spread domestic operations not already well known to the officials there. Seasoned administrators also develop a sixth sense anticipatory of citizen reactions.

Intelligence of this sort is much more informative and useful than either formal or informal hearings. Formal paper submissions are highly useful, even though more useful than informative. Hearings of informal character are primarily necessary for public-relations purposes. Indeed the chief common shortcomings of the administrative process in organizations otherwise highly elevated in quality of performance are in its public relations aspect. In spite of the concern and the effort of the public organizations, outgoing letters are often much less satisfactory than they should be. It is extremely difficult, of course, to bridge the wide gap between the interests of a particular citizen in a single situation and the requirements of system and the results of adjustment to great numbers of citizens differently conditioned. The business for which explanation is required is extremely complicated, and the expert character of those who write the letters of explanation detracts from their ability to communicate in simple, understandable terms. For somewhat similar reasons, scholars usually can publish only in learned journals, not in popular publications. It is true, too, of course, that experts too generally resent, and fail to react appreciatively even when yielding to, diverse citizen-political attitudes.

Part of what is not made clear to the public is not clear enough in the administrative process itself. It is a rather general but informal practice that complaints get attention at least one level higher than the level at which responsibility for the action complained about had been assumed, and that successive complaints are handled at successively higher levels. This practice occasions the most frequent of the activities of administrative review. There is too little consciousness of the practice, however, and it is not sufficiently consistent; too often initial criticisms are reviewed at the point, or below the point, where previous action had been determined. And too often the outgoing mail suggests that there has been less fresh and higher-level consideration of the matter than has actually been given it. These are illustrative of some of the needed and feasible improvements in the process. Even now, however, the dealing with public action in terms of current and prospective citizen reaction constitutes in bulk a very large part of the process of public administration. In the line hierarchy responsible for the conduct of public programs, the bulk is especially great. It bears indirectly through line agencies, on staff units.

It is in the consideration of this process of appeal and re view that the value-laden administrative process and the significance of a hard core of centralization emerge most vividly. It is only where and because there is a definite, hierarchal chain of command, reaching unbroken to the political heads of agencies, and to the President, the Congress, and the general public, that there can be general reliance on such a process and that it can be oriented toward the general public interest. More generally, it justifies Chester Barnard's statement in the *American Political Science Review:*

> The centralization of responsibility, which Americans seem to fear, permits and requires the delegation of responsibility and the magnifying of the moral forces by which, primarily, I think, bureaucracy can be controlled.

Thus responsibility, not authority, becomes, after politics, the key word in democratic public administration. It is politics that fashions and directs responsibility. It is hierarchy that is the formal structure and instrument of responsibility.

The process of democratic public administration is one of group judgment at each hierarchal level, judgment of groups of levels, group judgment subject to review, modification, revocation, and punitive action at any one of the many higher levels as consequences of the judgment's having come to bear upon citizens and having become subject to the reaction of citizens. It is a process in which facilities of appeal and levels of review are more numerous, various, and open than in any other action-laden process yet devised. It is a process carried on in an environment more critical and more politically active and potent than the environment of any other administrative process. It is a process in which the pattern of responsibility runs to public representativeness of many kinds and roles, to subordinates, to associates in the same unit, to contiguous and related units with somewhat different responsibilities, to higher executive levels where repose broader responsibilities; it runs outward to special publics, outward from higher levels to other and larger publics, outward and upward from executive agencies to the Chief Executive, to the Congress, and to the general public.

It is a pattern essentially unchanged from its original design, yet long under construction and now far developed in living action. What has been taking place in our government throughout its history is, in broad outline, simple—an extension in number of hierarchal levels. The extension reflects primarily two things: one is an extension in number of and dimensions of publics, their interests, and activities; the second is the associated extension of learnings, utilization of which requires taking them into account in carrying on affairs which in simpler times appeared to have simpler content. In other words, our government reflects the enrichment of our civilization. This may be the meaning of

Homans' sociological dictum that "civilization means centralization."

The administrative meaning of an extension in number of levels is an increase in delegation, with an accompanying requirement for improved techniques for co-ordination, review, and organization for controllability. Particular things Washington did as President soon came to devolve upon cabinet members; things done by cabinet members similarly were done by subordinate officials; things done by subordinates of that rank came to rest normally on desks of others lower in relative rank now elevated to higher absolute rank. In each case the delegation was essential to preservation and extension of the higher level responsibility. For a President today to attempt to handle the particular kinds of business dealt with personally by Washington would weaken that President and lead him to abysmal failure and the country to irresponsible chaos. The same thought applies at every executive level. It applies very especially at the legislative level. The congressional job has never been formally reclassified, but it has been moving successively to higher hierarchal positions; and its success is dependent upon its own recognition of its proper level, with suitable utilization of supporting, subordinate responsibilities.

Our governmental problems today should be no more difficult for us than they were for our forebears at the time of our national beginning, when nearly all had serious doubts about the feasibility of the bold new experiment. But our problems today require advanced understanding of institutions, and to attempt to solve them in terms of the old New England town meeting—which itself has greatly changed —would be like trying to use simple arithmetic for the solving of a problem in calculus. The course of civilization leads inevitably not only to higher mathematics but to higher and more complicated social and governmental forms.

The democratic, public-administrative process is an important part of the whole process of government. The entire process is one shaped by long years of experience and learning under the tutorial blows of publics and citizens sensitive, critical, and demanding. It is a process in which techniques unnumbered and often not consciously identified have been developed in harmony with the particular, evolving culture for which this process is both a present expression and an avenue for adjustment and advance. At any given time and in any jurisdiction it approximately embodies the administrative-political wisdom *effective* at that time in that jurisdiction.

THE ADMINISTRATIVE PROCESS

Public administration is a process steadily being improved under increasing attention, and ever capable of further improvement. Much of its improvement is technical and highly complicated business. Even such improvement cannot be had exclusively as a gift from experts, administrators or "the government"; there must be popular stimulation and effective support for it. Some other improvement is in a sense technical in nature but so broadly important as to require not merely popular support but popular understanding. The importance of a clear *capacity to review and intervene* at each higher hierarchal level in the executive branch is, perhaps, the most important of these broad, technical learnings. Adequate bridging between the expert and the civil service generally on the one hand, and the political officials on the other hand, is another. The importance of Congress reserving its powers for action appropriate to its level is another. Recognizing the reality and necessity of policy-making at all levels, if proposed improvements are to be constructive, is yet another. Identification of the excessive tendency toward "bloc" government and away from majority govern-

254 MORALITY AND ADMINISTRATION

ment is imperative. Central to all these is the strengthening
and elevation of political responsibility. Widespread understanding of these things will make possible many reforms.

Any attempted study of public administration which
would exclude illumination of such administration as at once
pursuing and deeply involved in values would be much less
than a study of public administration. This is peculiarly and
especially true when the study is directed at administration
in democratic government.

Similarly, any course in American government or any
general formulation of American political theory which fails
to comprehend and integrate into it the general administrative process (not merely the much less extensive legalistic
process) deals with much less than the putative subject. It
would deal largely with the effective inanimate.

Government and governmental theory find completion
beyond their terms of reference and beyond decisions to
act, in sequential actions. The whole administrative process
is the means by which government comes alive, and pursues
and helps give form and reality to values. Similarly, it gives
form and meaning to theory and provides functional materials out of which meaningful theory is created, tested,
and modified. The administrative process is the decision-
making, action part of the larger process of governance, deriving from it and flowing into it. Administration in this
broadest and most proper sense comprises the whole of governmental action, whether the action is "legislative," "executive," or "judicial." It is heightened recognition of this
that permits Professor Wallace Sayre to identify the most
significant drive of students of public administration as pursuit of a theory of government. In that theory, political responsibility must find new emphasis and refinement.

The value content of administration makes its process a
matter of grave importance, for process must to an extent

always symbolize and stand in lieu of values never to be precisely and finally defined apart from viable process. But too often the concern for good process has turned too exclusively on details abstracted from the whole process, and without sufficient appreciation of the larger value assurances and impediments in the larger process.

The administrative process is the continuing and developing performance of an orchestra. Under direction, using instruments designed and made by others, in a variety and number determined for them, the orchestra makes real in special arrangements conceptions of composers in form and character the composers could not fully know until their conceptions are thus brought to life. What is done reflects musical theory and in action provides materials for testing, modifying, and developing theory. The orchestra is capable of wide variations in direction, individual performances, sympathetic adjustments of members to each other, responsiveness to the opportunity provided by different compositions, the entire program arrangement, and audience perception and reaction.

"Eloquence," a teacher of speech used to say frequently, "is not an attribute of a speaker; it is a kind of electrical interchange between speaker and audience." So it is with this musical performance; its final reality and its meaning and value, dependent upon many factors, emerge only in the interaction of musicians and audience. The measure of "good" in government is possible—the very conception of government becomes meaningful—only as it emerges in action and there is interchange between acting government and acting citizens. Yet that interchange both derives from and contributes to the whole social scene. In observing the interchange it is well to discriminate between those of special privilege bemoaning a decrease in the frequency with which the numbers they request are played, and those who are critical because even now they have too little to do with determining the program.

Public administration in its narrowest useful sense—the conduct of "executive" government—may be viewed as having a specialized process, if we remember that it begins in and is pervaded by interaction with other aspects of government and with society.

The process derives importantly from Constitutional provisions, structural and other. But these provisions are necessarily and desirably more equivocal than most citizens realize. Judge Simon H. Rifkind not long ago pointed to a "basic Constitutional conflict" between the provision protective of free speech and free press, and the provision protective of trial procedures. Many political scientists have not failed to note the inconsistency between an apparent but not clearly enunciated separation of powers and other provisions for the President's leadership of Congress, his veto power, his pre-eminent role in foreign and military affairs, and his responsibility for general integrating leadership implicit in the role of Chief Executive. This latter role was immediately recognized and assumed by Washington. Many, on the other hand, have taken a general structural arrangement to mean much more than it could mean, to deny organic character to the government as a whole in unintended opposition to the meaning and necessity of the whole document. Persons thus sprinkled at the governmental fount but never immersed have failed to see the essence of living government as under political control in flexible use of these interrelated Constitutional arrangements in dynamic and reciprocal interaction between each other and their various sequential products.

The process is similarly and contextually based on law, not so much on any single law, apparently alone, specifically and precisely controlling and foretelling action, but on the interacting complex of laws, in the interstices of law, and on the extension of law requisite to its adjustable application. Equivocal meaning and inconsistency in Constitutional provisions, in particular laws and in the body of law are implicit in their dealing with many different values necessarily formulated in more or less abstract terms and dependent upon fulfillment in complementary and not automatic action. The subsequent and sequential actions, whether in judicial decision, further legislative enactment, or executive performance, are also more tentative, less precise and final, less meaningful when regarded apart from their flow and context, than orderly minds will be forever trying to make them.

Alongside and beyond Consitution and laws, the administrative process is derived from and contributory to politics —the politics of lawmaking, of judicial derivation and responsibility, of elections, of public sentiments in ebb and flow, of party, interest, and ideal forces operating everywhere in the relevant scene and not least on administrative officers and agencies. So derived, it partakes also of social and political history, tradition, custom, habit, mores, dynamics, culture.

In this context, under these influences and controls, and through the structures of the environing scene, the specialized process identifiable within the "executive" field is notably distinguished by these features:

1. A highly extended and specialized proliferation of hierarchy with many levels, requiring delegation and differentiation, and with complex interaction between its parts similar to the interaction between the executive branch and the conditioning structures and forces of its environment.

2. Within and associated with this hierarchal structure a formulation of group and organizational judgment bringing together the diverse fruits of human learning for technological application, multiplying value factors, and combining

and relating technical and value factors in action judgment.

3. Through hierarchal structure a process of review and appeal receptive to and treating intraorganizational reactions and citizen reactions to the organizational performance. This process of review and appeal, rooted particularly in a formal and central structure of control, is the complement of delegation, but it is more than that; it is the implementation of responsiveness in responsibility.

4. A vehicle for individual imaginativeness, for testing abstract thinking in individual terms, for contributions of values from formal and informal sources of leadership and responsibility. Here individual officials become a part of, as well as agents in, the administrative process. "Government by law" is not only impossible, but also inconceivable, except as it is also government by men. Within the executive branch as well as within the government at large, democratic government is government of, for, and by people, and only thus can be of, for, and by *the* people.

Perhaps no more specific or rigid description of the administrative process can be valid and applicable in the whole area of executive government. It may be that only because the process is so incapable of precise general description is it one in which continually and with reasonable acceptability it contributes to the casting of balances of very complicated and differentiated values. In the executive branch area as elsewhere must be weighed both *pluribus* and *unum;* in it as elsewhere must be weighed sympathy, compassion, magnanimity, equity, beauty, welfare and human unfolding along with order, defense, self-interest, bread, brick, and machines.

INDEX

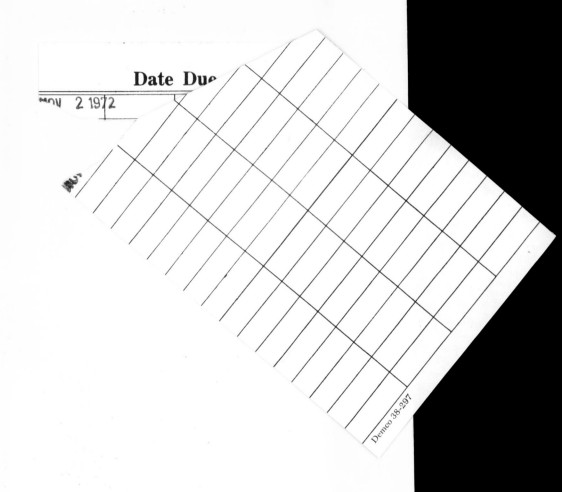